First World War
and Army of Occupation
War Diary
France, Belgium and Germany

21 DIVISION
64 Infantry Brigade,
Brigade Machine Gun Company
31 January 1916 - 31 January 1918

WO95/2162/3

The Naval & Military Press Ltd
www.nmarchive.com
Published in association with The National Archives

Published by

The Naval & Military Press Ltd

Unit 10 Ridgewood Industrial Park,

Uckfield, East Sussex,

TN22 5QE England

Tel: +44 (0) 1825 749494

www.naval-military-press.com

www.nmarchive.com

This diary has been reprinted in facsimile from the original. Any imperfections are inevitably reproduced and the quality may fall short of modern type and cartographic standards.

© Crown Copyright

Images reproduced by permission of The National Archives, London, England, 2015.

Contents

Document type	Place/Title	Date From	Date To
Heading	WO95/2162-3		
Heading	21st Division 64th Infy Bde 64th Machine Gun Coy. Jan 1916-Jan 1918		
Heading	On His Majesty's Service.		
Heading	War Diary Of 64th Machine Gun Company Commencing Jan 31st 1916 To March 31st 1916 Volume 1		
War Diary	Grantham	31/01/1916	24/02/1916
War Diary	Southampton	24/02/1916	24/02/1916
War Diary	Havre	25/02/1916	25/02/1916
War Diary	Southampton	25/02/1916	25/02/1916
War Diary	Havre	28/02/1916	28/02/1916
War Diary	Southampton	07/03/1916	07/03/1916
War Diary	Havre	02/03/1916	03/03/1916
War Diary	Abbeville	03/03/1916	03/03/1916
War Diary	Steenwerck	03/03/1916	04/03/1916
War Diary	Armentieres	04/03/1916	07/03/1916
War Diary	Houplines	08/03/1916	13/03/1916
War Diary	Armentieres	14/03/1916	19/03/1916
War Diary	La Creche	19/03/1916	20/03/1916
War Diary	Clapbanck	22/03/1916	30/03/1916
War Diary	Godewaersvelde	30/03/1916	30/03/1916
War Diary	Longueau	30/03/1916	31/03/1916
War Diary	Bonnay	31/03/1916	31/03/1916
Heading	War Diary Of 64 Machine Gun Company From April 1st 1916 To April 30th 1916 Volume I		
War Diary	Bonnay	01/04/1916	06/04/1916
War Diary	Ville	06/04/1916	06/04/1916
War Diary	Meaulte	07/04/1916	14/04/1916
War Diary	Ville	15/04/1916	15/04/1916
War Diary	Bonnay	15/04/1916	23/04/1916
War Diary	Ville	25/04/1916	30/04/1916
Heading	War Diary Of 64 Machine Gun Coy From May 1st 1916 To May 31st 1916 (Volume 3)		
War Diary	Ville	01/05/1916	02/05/1916
War Diary	Meaulte	02/05/1916	13/05/1916
War Diary	Ville	14/05/1916	14/05/1916
War Diary	La Neuville	14/05/1916	23/05/1916
War Diary	Ville	24/05/1916	31/05/1916
Heading	War Diary Of 64 Machine Gun Company From June 1st 1916 June 30th 1916		
War Diary	Meaulte	01/06/1916	11/06/1916
War Diary	Ville	12/06/1916	12/06/1916
War Diary	La Neuville	13/06/1916	20/06/1916
War Diary	Ville	21/06/1916	24/06/1916
War Diary	Buire	26/06/1916	30/06/1916
Map	Message Map		
Miscellaneous	Message Form		
Heading	64th Inf Bde 21st Div 64th Machine Gun Company July 1916		

Heading	War Diary Of 64 Machine Gun Coy From July 1st 1916 To July 31st 1916		
War Diary	Trenches E Of Becourt	01/07/1916	01/07/1916
War Diary	Sunken Rd.	02/07/1916	03/07/1916
War Diary	Assembly Trenches	03/07/1916	03/07/1916
War Diary	Dernancourt	04/07/1916	04/07/1916
War Diary	Ailly-Sur Somme	04/07/1916	04/07/1916
War Diary	Yzeux	05/07/1916	07/07/1916
War Diary	Fourdrinoy	07/07/1916	10/07/1916
War Diary	Breuilly	10/07/1916	10/07/1916
War Diary	Ailly-Sur Somme	10/07/1916	11/07/1916
War Diary	Corbie Ville	11/07/1916	12/07/1916
War Diary	Bottom Wood	13/07/1916	15/07/1916
War Diary	Bazentin Le-Petit Wood	16/07/1916	17/07/1916
War Diary	Ailly-Sur Somme. Longeau	23/07/1916	23/07/1916
War Diary	St Pol	23/07/1916	23/07/1916
War Diary	Berlencourt	23/07/1916	28/07/1916
War Diary	Wanquetin	28/07/1916	28/07/1916
War Diary	Arras	28/07/1916	28/07/1916
War Diary	Duisans	29/07/1916	29/07/1916
War Diary	Arras	29/07/1916	31/07/1916
War Diary		17/07/1916	17/07/1916
War Diary		01/07/1916	01/07/1916
Miscellaneous	21st Division.	21/07/1916	21/07/1916
Heading	64th Brigade Machine Gun Company August 1916		
War Diary	Arras	02/08/1916	30/08/1916
Heading	64th Brigade Machine Gun Company September 1916		
Heading	Original War Diary 64th Machine Gun Company From 1 Sept 1916 to 27th Sept 1916 Vol 7		
War Diary	Arras	01/09/1916	03/09/1916
War Diary	Duisans	04/09/1916	04/09/1916
War Diary	Ilez-Les-Hameau	04/09/1916	11/09/1916
War Diary	Canettemont	12/09/1916	12/09/1916
War Diary	Dernancourt	13/09/1916	14/09/1916
War Diary	Fricourt Camp	15/09/1916	15/09/1916
War Diary	Pommiers Redt	16/09/1916	16/09/1916
War Diary	Flers	17/09/1916	17/09/1916
War Diary	Pommiers Camp	18/09/1916	18/09/1916
War Diary	Fricourt Camp	19/09/1916	22/09/1916
War Diary	Bernafay Wood	23/09/1916	24/09/1916
War Diary	Guedecourt	25/09/1916	26/09/1916
War Diary	Bernafay Wood	27/09/1916	30/09/1916
War Diary	Ribemont	01/10/1916	02/10/1916
War Diary	Monfliers	03/10/1916	07/10/1916
War Diary	Burbure	08/10/1916	10/10/1916
Heading	War Diary Of 64th M.G.C. for month of October /16 Vol 8		
War Diary	Burbure	11/10/1916	12/10/1916
War Diary	Bethune	12/10/1916	16/10/1916
War Diary	Cambrin	17/10/1916	28/10/1916
War Diary	War Diary of 64 M.G. Coy. from 1st Nov to 30th Nov/16 Vol 9		
War Diary	Cambrin	04/11/1916	28/11/1916
War Diary	Bethune	29/11/1916	29/11/1916
Heading	64 M.G.Co. War Diary For December 1916 Vol 10		
War Diary	Bethune	29/11/1916	06/12/1916

War Diary	Vermelles	14/12/1916	31/12/1916
War Diary	Noeux Les Mines	01/01/1917	19/01/1917
War Diary	Fouquereuil	20/01/1917	20/01/1917
War Diary	Noeux Les Mines	22/01/1917	27/01/1917
War Diary	Chocques	28/01/1917	28/01/1917
War Diary	Esquelbeck	29/01/1917	29/01/1917
War Diary	La Motte	31/01/1917	10/02/1917
War Diary	Bethune	11/02/1917	11/02/1917
War Diary	Trenches	21/02/1917	28/02/1917
War Diary	Cambrin	01/03/1917	04/03/1917
War Diary	Bethune	05/03/1917	05/03/1917
War Diary	Robecq	06/03/1917	09/03/1917
War Diary	Mazingham	10/03/1917	11/03/1917
War Diary	Pressy-Les-Pernes	12/03/1917	12/03/1917
War Diary	Framecourt	13/03/1917	13/03/1917
War Diary	Brevillers	14/03/1917	23/03/1917
War Diary	Grenas	24/03/1917	27/03/1917
War Diary	Berles-Les Bois	28/03/1917	28/03/1917
War Diary	Bienvillers	30/03/1917	30/03/1917
War Diary	Boiry St Martin	01/04/1917	29/04/1917
War Diary	Hindenburg Line	01/05/1917	09/05/1917
War Diary	Bailleulval	11/05/1917	31/05/1917
War Diary	St Leger Boiry Becquerelle Road	31/05/1917	15/06/1917
War Diary	Boyelles	19/06/1917	19/06/1917
War Diary	Bienvillers	26/06/1917	29/06/1917
War Diary	Moyenville	30/06/1917	30/06/1917
War Diary	Moyenville Croisilles Rt Sector	01/07/1917	08/07/1917
War Diary	Moyenville	08/07/1917	08/07/1917
War Diary	Croisilles Left Sector	16/07/1917	16/07/1917
War Diary	Moyenville	24/07/1917	06/08/1917
War Diary	Bullecourt 51B S.W4	06/08/1917	20/08/1917
War Diary	Moyenville	25/08/1917	25/08/1917
War Diary	Boisleu-Au-Mont	26/08/1917	28/08/1917
War Diary	Bernecourt	28/08/1917	28/08/1917
War Diary	Scottish Wood	30/09/1917	30/09/1917
War Diary	Glencorse Wood	03/10/1917	04/10/1917
War Diary	Trench	04/10/1917	07/10/1917
War Diary	Polygon	02/10/1917	03/10/1917
War Diary	Trenches	04/10/1917	07/10/1917
War Diary	Polygon	03/10/1917	03/10/1917
War Diary	Trenches	04/10/1917	07/10/1917
War Diary	Renescure	08/10/1917	21/10/1917
War Diary	Birr x Rds	21/10/1917	21/10/1917
War Diary	Clapham Junction	21/10/1917	22/10/1917
War Diary	In The Line	23/10/1917	28/10/1917
War Diary	Hallebast Corner	28/10/1917	03/11/1917
War Diary	In The Line	03/11/1917	12/11/1917
War Diary	Anzac Camp	13/11/1917	13/11/1917
War Diary	Ottawa Camp Ouderdum	14/11/1917	17/11/1917
War Diary	Doulieu	17/11/1917	17/11/1917
War Diary	La Couronne	18/11/1917	19/11/1917
War Diary	Vendin	19/11/1917	21/11/1917
War Diary	Mont St Eloi	21/11/1917	30/11/1917
War Diary	Tincourt	01/12/1917	02/12/1917
War Diary	Heudicourt	02/12/1917	10/12/1917
War Diary	Longavesnes	10/12/1917	12/12/1917

War Diary	Heudicourt	12/12/1917	22/12/1917
War Diary	Left Sector	22/12/1917	31/12/1917
War Diary	Heudicourt	31/12/1917	03/01/1918
War Diary	In The Line	04/01/1918	11/01/1918
War Diary	Line	11/01/1918	11/01/1918
War Diary	Heudicourt	11/01/1918	19/01/1918
War Diary	Left Sector	19/01/1918	27/01/1918
War Diary	Heudicourt	28/01/1918	31/01/1918
Heading	10th K.O.Y.L.I. Vol 6		
Heading	22nd Divl Train A.S.C. Sep-Oct 1915		

W0a5/2/62/3

21ST DIVISION
64TH INFY BDE

64TH MACHINE GUN COY.
JAN 1916 - JAN 1918.

On His Majesty's Service.

D.A.A.G.(I)
3rd Echelon

Officer i/c
6th Infantry Section
G.H.Q.
3rd Echelon

XXI
64th M.G. Coy
Vol 1

CONFIDENTIAL

War Diary.

of

64th Machine Gun Company

Commencing Jan 31st 1916 To March 31st 1916

(Volume 1)

Army Form C.2118.

WAR DIARY
or
INTELLIGENCE SUMMARY.
(Erase heading not required.)

Instructions regarding War Diaries and Intelligence Summaries are contained in F.S. Regs., Part II. and the Staff Manual respectively. Title pages will be prepared in manuscript.

Place	Date	Hour	Summary of Events and Information	Remarks and references to Appendices
GRANTHAM.	31/1/16		The Company commenced mobilization	G.H.C.
GRANTHAM	18/2/16	11.30 am	Inspection by G.O.C. M.G.T.C.	G.H.C.
"	24/2/16	3.25 am	Company left GRANTHAM Station; all personnel and equipment correctly entrained.	G.H.C.
SOUTHAMPTON	"	12 noon	Arrived & detrained. Company split into two parties; 1st party & officers 71 O.R., horses, mules & transport embarking on the "Archimedes"; 2nd party 5 officers 70 O.R. embarking on the "Hacquerita". 2nd party sailed on this night.	G.H.C.
HAVRE	25/2/16		2nd party disembarked & and proceeded to rest camp.	
SOUTHAMPTON	"		1st party still on board the "Archimedes"	G.H.C.
HAVRE	29/2/16		6231 Pte Dover G and 5439 Pte Whitman C. admitted to Hospital with Scabies	G.H.C.

Army Form C. 2118.

WAR DIARY
or
INTELLIGENCE SUMMARY.
(Erase heading not required.)

Instructions regarding War Diaries and Intelligence Summaries are contained in F. S. Regs., Part II and the Staff Manual respectively. Title pages will be prepared in manuscript.

Place	Date	Hour	Summary of Events and Information	Remarks and references to Appendices
SOUTHAMPTON	1/3/16	7.30 p.m.	1st Party sailed.	G.H.C.
HAVRE	2/3/16	9 a.m.	1st Party disembarked, & was joined by 2nd party in the afternoon.	
"	"	Midnight	Entrained at Gare Marchandise.	G.H.C.
"	3/3/16	3.20 a.m.	Left HAVRE.	
"	"	9 a.m.	Stopped for 1 an hour	
"	"	8.45 p.m.	Stopped for 1 an hour at	
ABBEVILLE	"	11.30 p.m.	Detrained in a snowstorm.	G.H.C.
STEENWERCK	"		Started on march to billets.	
"	4/3/16	3 a.m.	Arrived in billets. Roads cobbled and country flat and flooded.	
ARMENTIERES	"	6 "	The transport moved to PONT DE NIEPPE	
"	"	4.30 p.m.	Enemy shelled the town slightly.	G.H.C.
"	5/3/16	noon	Mens billets inspected by Brigade Commander.	G.H.C.
"	6/3/16	9 a.m.	D.C. Coy and Mess Officer & section went to the left sector of Brigade front. 5348 Pte Davis H. and Sykes H. G.H.C.	
"	"		Two men admitted to hospital.	
"	7/3/19	7 p.m.	Company relieved No 62 M.G. Coy in the Trenches. 5410 Pte Russell W & Shulter G to hospital	G.H.C.
HOUPLINES	8/3/19		System of 1 officer being relieved starts. 9 guns in the trenches, 6 in reserve.	
"	"		Drivers paid.	G.H.C.

WAR DIARY or INTELLIGENCE SUMMARY

(Erase heading not required.)

Army Form C. 2118.

Instructions regarding War Diaries and Intelligence Summaries are contained in F.S. Regs., Part II. and the Staff Manual respectively. Title pages will be prepared in manuscript.

Place	Date	Hour	Summary of Events and Information	Remarks and references to Appendices
HOUPLINES	10/3/16		No 1 Section relieved by No 3, No 3 guns of No 2 return relieved by 3 gun teams of No 4 section.	G.H.C.
"	11/3/16	6.30 p.m.	Two guns of No 1 Section fired indirect fire. Rounds expended 5,000. Targets: CHASTITY ST. & Tramway running due E of LES 4 HALLOTS FARM. Results not reported, but enemy retaliated in another part of the line.	G.H.C.
"	12/3/16 10.45 p.m.		Four guns of No 2 & 4 Sections fired indirect. Rounds expended 5,500. Targets 1. PARALLEL ST. 3. FRELINGHEIN CROSS RD. 2. L'AVENTURE RD. 4. Communication Trenches. Results unknown. It was reported that 1 man in the front line of our trenches was wounded by H.G. fire: this report was not substantiated. 5436 Cpl Draper (Madaurette) to hospital (insanity)	G.H.C.
"	13/3/16 7 p.m.		Company relieved by 62 M.G. Coy. Last party arrived in billets at ARMENTIÈRES at 11 p.m. 3633 Cpl Draper H evacuated to C.C.S. No 1. 5554 Pte Sykes evacuated to 15th C.C.S.	G.H.C.
ARMENTIÈRES	14/3/16		Gas helmet drill for the Company. 5352 Pte Marsh A admitted to hospital (scabies)	G.H.C.
"	15/3/16		Complete inspection of guns, kit, equipment etc. Defections by S.Os and deficiencies reported. Company was paid. No 1 & 2 Sections and HQ had baths. 5398 Pte Moser C. admitted to hosp	G.H.C.
"	16/3/16		No 3 & 4 Sections had baths. 5399 Pte Hawes evacuated to 2nd D.R.S.	G.H.C.
"	17/3/16		2/Lt G.A. Simpson: 6534 Cpl Trelor A; 6232 Cpl Sleent to admitted to hospital.	G.H.C.
"	19/3/16 10 a.m.		Company marched out of ARMENTIÈRES for divisional rest area.	G.H.C.
LA CRÈCHE	"	3 p.m.	Arrived in billets for the night at 3 p.m. Part of the road detailed for use in passing was found impassable. Bob.	G.H.C.

T2134. Wt. W708—776. 500000. 4/15. Sir J. C. & S.

WAR DIARY or INTELLIGENCE SUMMARY

Army Form C. 2118.

Place	Date	Hour	Summary of Events and Information	Remarks and references to Appendices
LA CRÈCHE	20/3/16	8 a.m.	Left billets and proceeded to CLAPBANCK, 1 mile S.W. of BAILLEUL billets at:	
CLAPBANCK	22/3/16		Company billeted in 3 farms. G.H.Q.	
			8 men from each of the following Bns. reported for training in Vickers Gun & were attached to Company for accommodation, rations and discipline - 1st E. Yorks Regt, 15th D.L.I.D	
"	23/3/16		10th K.O.Y.L.I. Attached to No 1, 2 & sections respectively. G.H.C.	
			8 men from 9th K.O.Y.L.I. reported for duty as above. Attached to No 3 Section.	
			5398 Pte Harrison S. discharged from hospital. G.H.C.	
"	24/3/16		6231 Pte Dodds W. and 6439 Pte Whitman C. struck off the strength of Company 29/3/16	G.H.C.
			Snowstorm prevented route march. Late Sections fitted their guns on miniature range.	
"	25/3/16		3411 2/Cpl Mayho H. admitted to Ross Field Ambulance. 5352 Pte Harwood discharged from hospital.	
			All mules and horses inoculated to Flanders. G.H.C.	
"	26/3/16		Two horses sent to mobile Vet Section No 33 for exchange.	
			Church Parade cancelled owing to rain. G.H.C.	
		7.30pm	4 reinforcements arrived. 26745 Pte Sanway D. 26746 Pte Sotten R. 26830 Pte Sheridan J. 13624 Pte Topp J. The 1st two posted to No 1 Section, Pte Sheridan to No 2 and Pte Topp to No 2 Section. G.H.C.	

WAR DIARY or INTELLIGENCE SUMMARY.

(Erase heading not required.)

Army Form C. 2118.

Place	Date	Hour	Summary of Events and Information	Remarks and references to Appendices
CLAPBANCR	27/3/16	2pm	Company pard. 5385 Pte Homen.W. @mitted to 2/4 E. Field Ambulance. G.H.C.	
"	28/3/16		Admitted 2/6 e Field Ambulance 5367 Pte Knot 5414 L/Cpl Haylor M. transferred from 6/6 F.D Amb & D.R.S. G.H.C.	
"	29/3/16	4.29p	5 men for batt'n attached for taining returned to town respective units. 5385 Pte Homen is discharged from hospital & the	
"	30/3/16		left billets and marched to GODEWAERSVELDE	
GODEWAESVELDE	30/3/16	7.30am	Entrained and at 10.30 a.m started fr LONGUEAU (Ref Sheet AMIENS 17. Sends 1/100,000)	
LONGUEAU	30/3/16	10.6pm	Arrived and detrained. G.H.C.	
	31/3/16	12.15am	Began march to billets at BONNAY.	
BONNAY	31/3/16	6am	Arrived. Billets proved insufficient for Men and horses: own accomodation taken was inspiring and the state of the roads during the march from LONGUEAU to BONNAY much better than that of those in the ARMENTIERES district. G.H.C.	

R.G.Bevan Capt.
O.C. 64 M.G. Coy.

64 M.G. Coy
Vol 2

CONFIDENTIAL

WAR DIARY

of

64 MACHINE GUN COMPANY.

VOLUME I

FROM APRIL 1st 1916
TO APRIL 30th 1916.

Army Form C. 2118.

WAR DIARY
or
INTELLIGENCE SUMMARY.
(Erase heading not required.)

Instructions regarding War Diaries and Intelligence Summaries are contained in F.S. Regs., Part II. and the Staff Manual respectively. Title pages will be prepared in manuscript.

Place	Date	Hour	Summary of Events and Information	Remarks and references to Appendices
BONNAY	1/4/16		5433 Cpl Draper H } struck off the Company. Invalided out of the Divisional Area. 5354 Pte Sykes H. }	
"	3/4/16		Cpl Draper from 12/3/16 and Pte Sykes from 6/3/16. G.H.C. Company paid. G.H.C.	
"	4/4/16		O.C. Coy, Lt ROBINSON and 2/Lt WATSON (visited) the Trench area to be occupied by the Brigade. G.H.C.	
"	6/4/16	7.30 a.m.	(horse) via HEILLY and BUIRE-SUR-L'ANCRE to VILLE-SUR-CORBIE (arrive) at CORBIE and parked transport. The horse lines very good. Ref. ALBERT {57D. S.E. 6² c. S.W. Continued {62D N.E. C2.c. N.W.	
VILLE	6/4/16	6.30 p.m.	Limbered wagons of 1, 3 and 4 sections with guards moved up to Dumps behind the trenches. No 1 Dump at F1.a.9.7; No 3 at F7.C.8t.3. Ref. TRENCH MAP. MEAULTE. 62D N.E.2. 1/10,000; No 4 at X.25.d.6.6 Ref. TRENCH MAP OVILLERS 57D S.E.4. 1/10,000. The contents of wagons were dumped under guard & the E-ns returned.	
"	"	7 p.m.	The Company moved up to MEAULTE and close hill(?) with the company (No 20 M.G. Coy) being relieved. G.H.C.	
MEAULTE	7/4/16	9 a.m.	Nos 1, 3 & 4 sections relieved No 20 M.G. Coy in the trenches. No 2 section was used as a fatigue party to assist the other sections in carrying up material to the gun emplacements.	
"	"	7.30 p.m.	20 M.G. Coy. moved out of the village. The 1st fighting limbers and S.A.A. carts of this Company brought up to Coy H.q.	

WAR DIARY or INTELLIGENCE SUMMARY

Army Form C.118.

Place	Date	Hour	Summary of Events and Information	Remarks and references to Appendices
MEAULTE	7/4/16	7.45pm	Ration cart by 2 limbered wagons Nos 1 & 3 having 1 limbered wagon, Nos 4, 7 & 8 & 27 Hg using the 3 ton. No transport is allowed to pass through the village without a pass from the C.R.E. G.H.C.	
"	8/4/16		5389 Pte Conwin W. (No 3 Sect) wounded in the arm by a rifle bullet. The careful censorship of all letters and the recent of hopes's secret the identity of the troops in this front emphasised by x Corps Commander in a letter of date 5/3/16. Two guns fired on HAMETZ – FRICOURT Rd and SAUSAGE SUPPORT About 2000 rds expended. No retaliation G.H.C. S.A.A	Ref MEAULTE Trench map 62D. N.E.2. BUXLLERS 57D S.E.4 G.H.C.
"	9/4/16		36,000 rounds drawn. Good rds were sent to No 1 by ration wagon in the night. 5 guns fired at WILLOW AVENUE – (1) BRANDY TRENCH – (2) SAUSAGE SUPPORT – (3) LOZENGE ALLEY – 1 gun enfilading road N.W. S.E. of RED COTTAGE. 8000 rds expended, no special retaliation which G.H.C. No 2 Section relieved No 3 in the trenches.	Ref maps an 8/4/16
"	10/4/16		5 Pts L Stelners's served out to the company. Iron Ration – 3 oz. cheese a platoon; half ration tin of a tin substitute for 1/3 of jammier a tin: The previous ration is regards as being more suitable for the company. Firing 6 guns: except that two guns fired at WILLOW AVENUE the targets were as for night.	G.H.C.

Army Form C. 18.

WAR DIARY
or
INTELLIGENCE SUMMARY.
(Erase heading not required.)

Instructions regarding War Diaries and Intelligence Summaries are contained in F. S. Regs., Part II. and the Staff Manual respectively. Title pages will be prepared in manuscript.

Place	Date	Hour	Summary of Events and Information	Remarks and references to Appendices
MEAULTE	11/4/16		Lewis Gun Cases taken over from 63 M.G. Coy. On receipt it was found they would not fit the guns when the light mountings is attached to them. The cases are therefore useless.	
"	"		3000 RDS sent to No 4 Section and 2000 to No 2.	
"	"	7 p.m.	A lively interchange of shells between our an the enemy's artillery. MEAULTE was not hit. Firing off of 6 on guns took place at the same targets as on night of 10/4/16. S.H.C.	
"	12/4/16		5393 Pte MILLS A.H. struck off the strength (to England) & sent to O.C. Reinforcements, M.G. Corps, Base Depot for despatch to England as under age. Authy. G.R. No 5544/29.31.	
			3000 RDS 1/5 MM drawn.	
			The need of more signallers was felt, and of was a great length of signal cable. It was found impossible to establish a reliable telephonic communication because owing to the shortage of cable, the line "cut in" to that of Bde Hqrs to 1st E. York Regt's HQ. S.H.C.	
"	13/4/16		1st fighting Limbers sent to Nos 1, 2 & 4 Sections. Dumps under a guard & remained all night.	
			The following were taken on the strength as reinforcements a/tty O.C. Reinforcements ETAPLES R.T. 199/1 ex d. 5/4/16	

WAR DIARY or INTELLIGENCE SUMMARY

Army Form C. 2118.

Place	Date	Hour	Summary of Events and Information	Remarks and references to Appendices
MEAULTE	13/4/16		11218 Pte PACE J.R.; 11245 Pte TRANTER W.; 11247 Pte TRANTER G.; 11250 Pte WILSON W.T. PACE, TRANTER & TRANTER posted to No 2 Sect. Pte WILSON & Pte TOONE to No 3. 3 Pte WILSON to No 4. There were no fatigues at the Coys. disposal.	
"	14/4/16		On 8/4/16 14218 The 8 men per Bn attached for training reported for duty. G.H.C. Relieved by 63 M.G. Coy. Relief Complete at 1 p.m. Company proceeded to VILLE except 2/Lts Milligan & Donnell left behind to supervise emplacements under construction by R.E. These two have arrived. G.H.C.	
VILLE	15/4/16	10 a.m.	Left VILLE for BONNAY.	
BONNAY	"	1 p.m.	Arrived here. Encountered a considerable amount of traffic en route; its weather again changed and squalls with intermittent sunshine made its roads very heavy. G.H.C.	
"	16/4/16		The day was spent in preparation for Brig. Gen's inspection. G.H.C.	
"	17/4/16	3 p.m.	Inspection by G.O.C. 64th Bde. The G.O.C. commanded the company's turn out. G.H.C.	
"	18/4/16		2/Lts Milligan & Donnell recalled. 5426 Dvr JEFFCOAT A.W. appointed A/ps L/cpl 16/4/16 G.H.C.	
"	19/4/16	21.00	Rns drawn from O.C. 63 M.G. Coy. Complete Team & 4 Gun Ratios. 2/Lt H.F.C. DONNELL transferred to Nos. 2 Section. 5320 Sgt GRANFT & 8091 Sgt MONEY W. Change places in Nos. 4 & 3 sections respectively. To date from 19/4/16	

WAR DIARY
or
INTELLIGENCE SUMMARY.
(Erase heading not required.)

Army Form C. 118.

Place	Date	Hour	Summary of Events and Information	Remarks and references to Appendices
BONNAY	19/4/16		5444 A/S/L/Cpl DUNN G. Dymoid of rank of L/Cpl.	E.H.C
"	20/4/16		Establishment. Lt AM Richardson reports this day having been transferred 67th Company from 9th R.Dy. L.I. as 2nd in command to complete establishment in accordance with A.G's A/6864 dated 9/4/16. Authy Fourth Army No A/2503 11/4/51 17/2/16.	
			5390 Pte Mc CUE taken on the strength as reinforcement 19/4/16. Authy O.C. Reinforcement ETAPLES R.T. 267/1	E.H.C
			A Divnl. Conference was held at LANEUVILLE at 2:30 pm. O.C. Cy attended.	E.H.C
"	22/4/16		Each Coy. by hand to VILLE.	E.H.C
VILLE	25/4/16		Lecture on + demonstration of gas poisons and lachymatry gases.	E.H.C
"	27/4/16		Gas Helmets used by Sections during tactical scheme. The Company's Gas Helmets + goggles inspected by M.O. in afternoon. The latter were condemned: No M.O officer recommends that an indent be submitted for "Rubber Sponge Goggles".	E.H.C
"	28/4/16	10 a.m.	Inspection by G.O.C. Divn. Another Divnl Conference was held in the afternoon at VILLE. 5444 Pte DUNN G. sent to N°4 Cy A.S.C. for instruction in C.B. shoeing. 3 trained farriers E.H.C.	
"	30/4/16	9.45 pm	Gas felt — Lachymatry stores and mules sent two miles further back.	

64 M.T. Cy

Capt.

64 MG
Vol 3

XX

CONFIDENTIAL

WAR DIARY

OF

64 Machine Gun Coy

(Volume 3.)

From May 1st 1916

To May 31st 1916

Army Form C.2118.

WAR DIARY
or
INTELLIGENCE SUMMARY.
(Erase heading not required.)

Instructions regarding War Diaries and Intelligence Summaries are contained in F.S. Regs., Part II. and the Staff Manual respectively. Title pages will be prepared in manuscript.

Place	Date	Hour	Summary of Events and Information	Remarks and references to Appendices
VILLE	1/5/16		5347 A/Cpl L/Cpl Wheatley H. Section No 1	
"	"		5342 " " " Golden a. " 2	Promoted Paid Act L/Cpls from 25/4/16
"	"		5367 " " " Zuile S. " 3	to complete establishment.
"	"		6399 " " " Powell a. " 4	
			Establishment by A.F.G.1098 - 203 April 1916 allows of another Officer, another	
			Artificer, another Horse (riding) and 1 Lance Sgt. and 5 Lance Corporals.	
			5407 Pte Hill C. appointed L/Cpl 29/4/16.	
			5325 M/CSM Geoge W: 5332 Cpl Thomas J.W.: 5339 Cpl Miles J: 5419 L/Cpl Chadwick G.	
			8954 Pte Cahill T: 8555 Pte Charles J: 8807 Pte Crowe V: 5382 Pte Joyce L:	
			5380 Pte Matthews A: 8242 Pte Shaw H. These N.C.O's & Men were returned	
			to M.G. Corps Depot at the Base in accordance with AG's A/6584 dated 8/4/16.	
			They were struck off the strength to-day.	
			5331 Sgt Betsworth E appointed A/CSM from to-day.	
			5342 L/Cpl Golden A. promoted Cpl " " "	
			5365 Pte Wright T. appointed L/Cpl/Act/L/Cpl " " "	
			L-Cos of Nos 2, 3 & 4 Sections sent to the Dumps formerly possessed by Nos 4, 1 & 2 respectively. G.H.C.

WAR DIARY
of
INTELLIGENCE SUMMARY.
(Erase heading not required.)

Army Form C. 2118.

Place	Date	Hour	Summary of Events and Information	Remarks and references to Appendices
VILLE	2/5/16	1.30 a.m.	No 2, 3 & 4 set off for the trenches: No 3 had also 1 gun team from No 7 Section	
		6.30 a.m.	Remainder of No 7 & trp set out for MEAULTE.	
MEAULTE	"	12 noon.	Relief of No 62 M.G. Coy in the trenches complete.	
			The following N.C.O.s & men are transferred from this date until provision of P.Reg's C.Etc.	
			A/68614 0 9/4/16	To Section
			12146 Sgt. Wilson J. 10th K.O.Y.L.I.	No 1.
			16770 Pte Hilliard T. 15th Durh. L.I.	No 2.
			17270 " Chilton H. "	"
			15930 " Walker C.S. "	"
			11407 " Dutton I. 9th K.O.Y.L.I.	No 3
			14035 " Gearly J. "	"
			14170 " Inden J. "	"
			19038 " Pope A. "	"
			1562 " Silvester F. "	" EHC
"	3/5/16	8.30 pm.	6 shells burst near Coy H.Q. 5390 Pte McCue slightly wounded.	S. HC
"	4/5/16	6.0 a.m.	3 more shells burst in the village. 19672 Pte Bartley D 1st E.York Regt (5th Battery D attached)	

Army Form C.2118.

WAR DIARY
or
INTELLIGENCE SUMMARY.
(Erase heading not required.)

Place	Date	Hour	Summary of Events and Information	Remarks and references to Appendices
MEAULTE	4/5/16		Pte 8605 Rabbetts.h. slightly wounded. Reports night firing	
	4/5/16		No 2. Gun Pos. X 26. C.18 (DRILLERS Trench hoop 57D.S.E.4.) Target. LOZENGE	
			TRENCH & ROUND WOOD (" " "). 8000 Rds expended.	
	4/5/16		No 3. Gun Pos. F.2.C.33 (MEAULTE " " 62.D. N.E.2.). Target German Trench 82-29.	
			2000 Rds expended. BRANDY TRENCH.	
			No 4. Target WILLOW AVENUE Rds expended 2000.	
	5/5/16		1 Gun & No 3 section disposed a limbing party during the day. Night much quieter. Ditto.	
			20019 Pte DUCE J.H. ⎫	
			22629 " OATES T.W. ⎬ attached from 9th K.O.Y.L.I. 6th to Coy for	
			17592 " GOGGAN. J. ⎬ training.	
			13639 " FOWLER J.W. ⎬	
			21206 " BATH C. ⎬	
			19955 " OUTRAM J.B. ⎬	
			17591 " VASEY. H. ⎬	
			19043 " MIDDLETON E. ⎭	
"	6/5/16		The undr promoting to Act Pd L/cpls. ⎧ 5847 Act L/cpl L/cpl Wratley H ⎫ is cancelled	
			⎨ 5357 " " Foster. S. ⎬	
			⎩ 5899 " " Hurll. A ⎭	

Army Form C. 2118.

WAR DIARY
or
INTELLIGENCE SUMMARY.
(Erase heading not required.)

Place	Date	Hour	Summary of Events and Information	Remarks and references to Appendices
MEAULTE	5/5/16		Firing. 2 Guns from position X.26.C.1.7 fired 1000 rds each at RAILWAY COPSE (BVILLERS TRENCH MAP) A German Machine Gun retaliated by firing at the CHATEAU; its position was estimated at X.26.6.6.1. 1 Gun fired 2000 rds at LOZENGE WOOD (ref MEAULTE TRENCH MAP): no retaliation was drawn. G.HC.	
"	6/5/16		Firing. One gun from T.8.6.5.2 (MEAULTE Trench Map) fired 8000 rds between 8pm and 12.30 a.m. (7/5/16) at LOZENGE WOOD. Germans opened fire with artillery at 9pm for 20 minutes but failed to hit the gun position. G.HC.	
"	7/5/16		No 1 Section relieved No 4 in the right sector; No 2 and 3 Sections changed places, in the left and centre sectors respectively. Firing. One gun from T.2.C.33 (MEAULTE Map) fired 2000 rds into SODA TRENCH and neighbourhood. One Gun from T.8.6.2.5 (MEAULTE Map) fired 2000 rds at LOZENGE WOOD and dug in to south of the wood. Two guns from X.76.C.1.8 fired 2000 rds each at railway near RAILWAY COPSE and reached the neighbourhood. G.HC.	

Army Form C. 2118.

WAR DIARY
or
INTELLIGENCE SUMMARY.
(Erase heading not required.)

Place	Date	Hour	Summary of Events and Information	Remarks and references to Appendices
MEAULTE	8/5/16		Firing. Two guns from X.26.c.18 fired 3,500 rds at French Railway near RAILWAY COPSE. Gasgun rd French troops DRILLENS. One gun from F.2.c3.3. (Trench Map MEAULTE) fired 2000 rds at S of A TRENCH neighbourhood. One gun from F.6.b.2.5 fired 2000 rds at LOZENGE WOOD I dug into S of the WOOD. At about 9pm fire was opened upon enemy dump N.E. of BOIS FRANCAIS from a disused position in SURREY ST. (Trench map MEAULTE). Hindrance in the vicinity was also searched. 750 rds being expended. E.H.C.	
"	9/5/16		3 wires were reported at 6 a.m. The M Guns Commanding Lieut. M. ROUR was warned, but it was not found necessary to reply empty the guns. 5381 Pte Curad.W. invalided R.R.R. 20/4/16 & struck off the strength of the Coy 9/4/16. 33094 Pte Gray T.A. (signaller) taken to strength from 19/5/16. E.H.C.	
"	10/5/16		Firing. M.Guns were very active during the night. Targets engaged - Trenches & Dump near BOIS FRANCAIS; Emplacements in trench in front of FRICOURT WOOD (MEAULTE MAP). There was considerable enemy M.G. fire all night in Southern portion of our line. E.H.C.	

Army Form C. 2118.

WAR DIARY
or
INTELLIGENCE SUMMARY.
(Erase heading not required.)

Place	Date	Hour	Summary of Events and Information	Remarks and references to Appendices
MEAULTE	11/5/16		Two guns fired during the night. Targets engaged :- LOZENGEWOOD, Trenches in front of FRICOURT WOOD. (Trench Maps MEAULTE & WILLERS) 1st Field GSOO. The enemy has been searching for two guns firing from BECOURT WOOD with shrapnel, but so far unsuccessfully. L/tc.	
	12/5/16		Relieved by 63 M.G. Coy. Relief complete 11 am. The Coy. marched @ VILLE-SUR-ANCRE (Medal FRANCE SHEET 62 D NE (Ed 2)) where the night was spent. L/tc. MEAULTE	
VILLE	13/5/16 10 am		March to LA NEUVILLE (AMIENS 1/100,000) commenced in rainstorm, which continued until short intervals until arrival.	
LA NEUVILLE			Arrived 2 pm and Distillers into Billets. L/tc.	
	14/5/16		Brigade Church Parade. 5645 Pte Milton J. attached to MSD. workshops & Corps (transit in repairing Corps late cart for return to etc.	
	15/5/16		Kit Inspection. 25109 Pte Thomas H. 839 Pte Haigh D. 2137 Pte Hitching R (9th G. Oy L.I.) returned to their R.R. as inefficient & unlikely to make Gun M. Gunners. etc.	

WAR DIARY or INTELLIGENCE SUMMARY

Army Form C. 2118.

(Erase heading not required.)

Place	Date	Hour	Summary of Events and Information	Remarks and references to Appendices
LA NEUVILLE	15/5/16		During period Wednesday 10/5/16 to Tuesday 16/5/16 the discrepancy in issue of meat was 10D ration short. 5602 W/S/L/Cpl Walsh R. deprived of Act. rank.	G.H.C.
"	16/5/16	am	Route March 9am to 1pm. Weather very hot.	G.H.C.
"	17/5/16	9-12.30	Tactical Scheme by ½ companies with Transport.	
"			16184 Pte HALL G.J. attd from 15th D.L.I. for training & complete 6 men 26039 " PUGH R.] Pte Bts attached to this Coy.	G.H.C.
"	18/5/16	6.9-12.30	Tactical Scheme by ½ companies with Transport.	G.H.C.
"	19/5/16	9am-12.30	Practice Attack on Trenches. These Trenches are a copy of the German Trenches facing Running from X.20.d. & 7.3. (Pt 72) to X.26.6.7. (Ref. FRANCE Sheet 57 D S.E. Ed. 2.A.) Orders for Packs to be worked received. A capital letter indicates a Bn. In the complete & separate unit, and a small letter the Company. This Coy will bear letter E : each section will bear small letters respectively as follows No.1, "a" ; No.2, "b" ; No.3, "c" ; No.4 "d" ; Tpt "f". Stop uniform & train sections.	
			Appointments & promotions. 5257 W/S/Sgt Foster S. to be paid A/Cpl 25/4/16 A/Cpl 18/5/16 to complete establishment G.H.C. 5602 " " " HILL C. 2/5/16 " " " 5607 " " Boxing Competition L/Cpl JEFFCOAT (asked for 7tho was beaten in semifinal after winning)	

WAR DIARY
or
INTELLIGENCE SUMMARY
(Erase heading not required.)

Army Form C. 2118.

Instructions regarding War Diaries and Intelligence Summaries are contained in F. S. Regs., Part II and the Staff Manual respectively. Title pages will be prepared in manuscript.

Place	Date	Hour	Summary of Events and Information	Remarks and references to Appendices
LA NEUVILLE	20/5/16	9am	Coy took part in Bde Attack on some trenches and the attack was practised in 3 days. A demonstration of Stokes Guns was given	
		5.30pm	Competition for prize of 80 frs given by G.O.C. 66th Inf Bde by Sections. Competition took form of "coming into action" & "getting out of action" from limbered wagons. Winners No 2 Section, not a good record. Prize (in cocoa) by Officers of Coy - £1 160 frs. In the course of this competition 16779 Pte EATON H (No 1 Section) was run over by a G.S. limber & seriously injured. Pte sent to the base.	
"	23/5/16	7am	Moved to FILLE arriving 10.15 am	
VILLE	24/5/16		The Company supplied a working party of 20 men	
			8 reinforcements reported & taken on strength of Coy 24/5/16. 26362 Pte HODGSON H. 14307 Pte SIMPSON R 14478 Pte WILLIAMS JENKINS G. 14471 Pte Jenkins G. 28068 " SLOANE G. 14314 " COX A.S. 14495 " Brownlow G. 28071 " Retd H. 9AC	
"	25/5/16		Establishment increased by 1 Riding horse for Tpt Sgt., 2 spare Draught horses and 1 spare driver.	
			The Coys Mark on the shoulder is an oval of green cloth, about 2½" long & 1¼" at widest part.	

Army Form C. 2118.

WAR DIARY
or
INTELLIGENCE SUMMARY.
(Erase heading not required.)

Instructions regarding War Diaries and Intelligence Summaries are contained in F.S. Regs., Part II. and the Staff Manual respectively. Title pages will be prepared in manuscript.

Place	Date	Hour	Summary of Events and Information	Remarks and references to Appendices
VILLE	27/5/16		12146 Sgt Watson F.9. 5536 Cpl Mason L. detailed to attend a 4 days course of instruction at Anti-Gas School, 20" Divl Working Parties as usual. Etc.	
"	28/5/16		Coml of Enquiry held on a lost bicycle. Marking of packs. Packs marked in this Coy as follows. Coy Letter E. No 1 Sect ... a ; No 2 Sect ... b ; No 3 Sect ... c ; No 4 Sect ... d ; Tpt ... t. HQ marked with their sections letters to to be put underneath. To pack between its supporting straps. Another working party provided. Trench m.g. emplacements 7pm – 1.30 am. Etc.	
"	29/5/16 30/5/16		Preparations for relieving 62 M.G. Coy in the trenches begun. Guns and material (all sections taken to dumps & left under a guard. Etc.	

A.S.Swan Capt.
Ot. 62 M.G. Coy.

CONFIDENTIAL

WAR DIARY

OF

64 MACHINE GUN COMPANY

From June 1st 1916 to June 30th 1916.

WAR DIARY or INTELLIGENCE SUMMARY

Army Form C. 2118.

Place	Date	Hour	Summary of Events and Information	Remarks and references to Appendices
MEAULTE	1/6/16	4 a.m.	Sections moved into the trenches & relieved 62 M.G. Coy. Relief complete at 10 a.m. All guns in the trenches (this period).	
"	2/6/16		Firing was carried out on the fire points in the German wire, taken by our Artillery in preparation of a raid by us, in order to prevent the enemy repairing this barbed wire.	
"	3/6/16		The same as previous night. The Germans made a raid on our Lt. Two Lewis Guns fired at enemy parapet in neighbourhood of PT 72 between 10 & 2.30 am when the enemy was trying to attack. 10 am guns at X.26.D.2.6 kept up fire on enemy front & sides of tents, where the engagement of infantry was in progress. A 9 inch Field Battery stationed in Fricourt hindered the enemy. Lt. A.N. RICHARDSON.	
"	4/6/16		Artillery bombardment by Germans about 9 pm. Our Artillery starting at 10.18 p.m. kept up barrage on enemy wire to our home in preparation of a raid by us. The Coy's machine guns' main duty was to cover the flanks of the raiding party. The raid was not made. Lt Robinson was (wm.) by an explosive shell (& injured). No 4 Section was also (wm.) (& dug out again. & resumed firing.	Raid was between E3.c.b.9.36 E.3.c.65.55 5 guns fired 1 gun in Enemy was 3 on Lt flank bombarded after 3 Rt Flank raid with two Lewis Guns X.20.a 10.2.6 &c.
"	5/6/16		A Raid by us took place against LA - BOISSELLE and our Machine Guns kept under fire the system of Trenches running from 20.a. 10.2. to 20.a. 9.3.	

Army Form C. 2118.

WAR DIARY
or
INTELLIGENCE SUMMARY.
(Erase heading not required.)

Instructions regarding War Diaries and Intelligence Summaries are contained in F.S. Regs., Part II. and the Staff Manual respectively. Title pages will be prepared in manuscript.

Place	Date	Hour	Summary of Events and Information	Remarks and references to Appendices
MEAULTE	7/6/16		Machine Guns very quiet ing to working parties. German working Party was again Down at F.9.6.8.2. and again dispersed by machine gun fire which also searched this forward trenches between 230 pm & midnight	
" "	8/6/16		Routes for traffic carrying ratios altered. From 22.a.7.3 (CHIMNEY) N.R. Road goes across the fits 16th SE of MEAULTE to 18.a.5.4, then CARCAILLOT FARM – BECOURT WOOD. (Trench Map MEAULTE 62.D N.E.2.) No Machine Guns fired and the day & night were normal.	
" "	9/6/16		Route for traffic going to BECOURT WOOD altered again to usual route via MEAULTE and ALBERT (MEAULTE 62.D N.E.2.) Firing in retaliation for cutting our wires on G on M. Guns fired 1570 SAA at 3.c N.W. 6.9.55. (MEAULTE Trench Map). Effects are not known: no retaliation was offered.	
" "	10/6/16		Company relieved in the trenches by 63 Machine Gun Coy. Relief complete by 10.30 am. Company marched to VILLE (ALBERT SHEET (Cambrai) /57D. S.E. 57c.S.W. & H.C. 62.D N.E. 62.C N.W.	

T2131. Wt. W708–776. 500000. 4/15. Sir J.C.&S.

WAR DIARY or INTELLIGENCE SUMMARY.

(Erase heading not required.)

Army Form C. 2118.

Place	Date	Hour	Summary of Events and Information	Remarks and references to Appendices
VILLE	12/6/16		Coy marched to LA NEVILLE to rest. Arrived at 2pm.	Gtc.
LA NEVILLE	13/6/16		Wash day and a general clean up. Inspection of all arm material, kit and equipment by section officers. Company was inspected by O.C. Coy in the afternoon. 11409 PTE DUTTON. T. struck off the strength of Coy 1/5/16 Gtc.	
" "	14/6/16		Coy took part in practice attack by the Brigade on the training trenches W. of LA NEVILLE. (Tracing trenches are copy of German 1st line system from PT 72 BENZEMIN X.20.a.7.2.5. and PT 78 X.26.a.7.8. Ref. FRANCE Sheet 57D S.E. Edition 2A.) Coy's distinguishing mark is a green oval, worn on both shoulders and the back. Machine of Packs. Coy's letter in E. No 1, 2, 3 the sections have a "a", "b", "c" 2"d" respectively on the Divisor 6". Each man has a number, the elevenths are in no 2 Sect bring "E.6.11." This is due to purposes of his'ing packs in the event of an advance.	Gtc.
" "	15/6/16		Another attack was carried out as to yesterday by the Brigade, but Coy did n't take part. Route march from 9am — 4pm. Dinners were cooked in the field	

Army Form C. 2118.

WAR DIARY
or
INTELLIGENCE SUMMARY.
(Erase heading not required.)

Instructions regarding War Diaries and Intelligence Summaries are contained in F.S. Regs., Part II. and the Staff Manual respectively. Title pages will be prepared in manuscript.

Place	Date	Hour	Summary of Events and Information	Remarks and references to Appendices
LA NEUVILLE	15/6/16		2/Lt F.E. TRANTER w/pokd arrival & is taken on strength p'day from this date.	
"			37766 Cpl MILLWARD W.E. (Saddler) taken on strength p'cay from this date. This was attnd. 12 midnight night 14–15/6/16	
"			became 1am 15/6/16.	
"			Lt B.S. ROBINSON wounded B.V.R. & shewn Robinson story 9/6/16	
"			4284 Sjt WINTER T.E. — " — 21/5/16	
"			5407 L/Cpl HILL C. — " — 28/5/16	
"	15/6/16		3/Lt H.T.C. DONNELL appointed to command MG Section vice Lt B.S. ROBINSON from this date.	Etc
"	16/6/16		Open warfare & return from trenches carried out by Sections in the morning: stoppages, care & cleaning (1 ransfixing etc carried out in the afternoon).	
"			All ranks wear HD of the coming British Offensive and part they are to play	
"			2/Lt G.A. SIMPSON returned to duty from Hospital	Etc
"			All ranks had notes to Sjt Louis closely supp'd.	
"	17/6/16		Bde Elizabeth...son in the attack. N.G. Coy for part the attack	
"			was in the training lectures to 47th NEUVILLE.	G.t.c

WAR DIARY
or
INTELLIGENCE SUMMARY

Army Form C. 2118.

Place	Date	Hour	Summary of Events and Information	Remarks and references to Appendices
LA NEUVILLE	18/6/16		B'dr Church Parade.	
"	19/6/16		Coy name of Coy changed to "B" STAR SPY. B'dr C.O. named SPAR. Coy cooperated with 15th Bn K.O.Y.L.I. in an attack in the training area. A practice enemy attack was witnessed. Conference of Coy Officers at 9pm.	Div'l operation orders for attack were discussed
"	20/6/16	11.45	hand to VILLE. The Kite Balloon was being shelled as coy entered KILLE. Arrived in billets at 2pm. Conference of Coy officers at 9pm at NeuvalVILLE.	
VILLE	21/6/16		Section work. Conference of coy officers at 9pm. B'de operation orders for the attack on the German Trenches were read & discussed. (B'de H'dqs Division Brigade operation orders will be submitted in this Diary later.)	
"	22/6/16		Conference of the Battalion Commanders to O.C. M.G. Coy held at 2.35pm at B'de H.Q. Conference of Coy officers at 9pm.	
"	23/6/16		The following were transferred from B.Coy in the Brigade (see War Diary for May) have been allotted M.G. Corps numbers as follows:—	
			Pte Glasby T 22116, Pte Pape A 22119, Sgt Colom T 22115	
			" Tawser T.D 22117, " Wallis C.S 22122, " Chicken H 22121	
			" Buckle W 22118, " Millward T 22120	
			22118 TPR BICKLE W taken for strength of Coy 2/6/16.	

WAR DIARY
or
INTELLIGENCE SUMMARY

Army Form C. 2118.

(Erase heading not required.)

Place	Date	Hour	Summary of Events and Information	Remarks and references to Appendices
VILLE	2/6/16		1562 Sergt Silvester is not transferred being a Special Reservist on transfer struck off strength of Coy from 2/6/16.	
VILLE	12/6/16	10am	Orders by G.O.C. 20th Divn. to 9th K.O.Y.L.I. D. This Company on the coming attack.	
"	"	12 noon	Inspection of Coy and Transport by G.O.C. 61st Inf. Bde. This remarks were as follows (extracts) 1. "On the whole very well turned out." 2. "Men are not sufficiently steady in the ranks & equipment was spread." 3. "Transport animals & wagons are in a good state."	
"	23/6/16		3/57 Pte MITCHEL G.J. (spare driver) taken on strength 21/6/16. Conference of Coy Officers.	
"	24/6/16		All materiel to Coy dumped & Salvage dumped near the Church in VILLE. Coy deposits Leather Boxes, Trench howitzers, Metallic Belts etc. Both Boys & Belts have been no use to the Coy - the first will not evolve a Gun where the light mounting is fixed to it. The bombardment of enemy trenches began in the afternoon. This was U Day. 16779 Pte EATON H is struck off the strength of the Coy from 14/6/16. Coy went into bivouac at BUIRE. Guns taken up to the trenches and put in the dug outs to be occupied by the Gun Teams during the night preceding the attack. V Day	
BUIRE	25/6/16			

WAR DIARY
or
INTELLIGENCE SUMMARY.
(Erase heading not required.)

Army Form C. 2118.

Place	Date	Hour	Summary of Events and Information	Remarks and references to Appendices
BULRE	26		W day.	
	27		X day 28th Y.	
	29/6/16		It was notified that the attack on the German Trenches would be cancelled on the 29th (Z day) inst, but was later postponed for 48 hrs – all units receiving the order to stand fast. So that the 30th June became Y day & July 1st Z day.	
" "	30/6/16		Company moved into the dug outs in the trenches alongside B"	
" "			Transport moved – A ECHELON (G.S. Limbered wagons, water carts) to E D VILLE B " (G.S. Wagons, Cook's cart etc.) to W of VILLE	
			Late on July 1st A ECHELON moved for the E and near MEAULTE.	

A.W. Keevan Capt
O.C. 64 M.G. Coy.

MESSAGE FORM.

To:—   No.

1. I am at......................... {Note:—Either give Map Reference or mark your position by a 'X' on the Map on back.

2. I have reached limits of my Objective.

3. My Platoon / Company is at...........................and is consolidating.

4. My Platoon / Company is at........................... and has consolidated.

5. Am held up by (a) M.G. (b) Wire at........................(Place where you are).

6. Enemy holding strong point..................

7. I am in touch with............................on Right / Left at............

8. I am not in touch with............................on Right / Left.

9. Am shelled from....................

10. Am in need of:—

11. Counter Attack forming at........................

12. Hostile (a) Battery
    (b) Machine Gun   active at........................
    (c) Trench Mortar

13. Reinforcements wanted at..

14. I estimate my present strength at...........rifles.

15. Add any other useful information here:—

                                                    Name........................
                                                    Platoon......................
Time................m.   Company....................
Date.............1917.   Battalion....................

———

(A). Carry no maps or papers which may be of value to the Enemy.

(B). Give no information, if captured, except the following, which you are bound to give:—
        Name and Rank.

(C). Collect all captured maps and papers and send them in at once.

64th Inf.Bde.
21st Div.

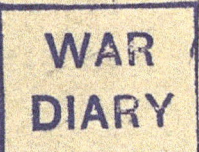

64th MACHINE GUN COMPANY.

J U L Y

1 9 1 6

CONFIDENTIAL.

WAR DIARY

OF.

64 MACHINE GUN COY.

from JULY 1st 1916.

to JULY 31st 1916.

Army Form C.2118.

WAR DIARY
or
INTELLIGENCE SUMMARY.
(Erase heading not required.)

Instructions regarding War Diaries and Intelligence Summaries are contained in F. S. Regs., Part II and the Staff Manual respectively. Title pages will be prepared in manuscript.

Place	Date	Hour	Summary of Events and Information	Remarks and references to Appendices
Trenches E of BECOURT WOOD	1/7/16	7.30	Z.o. (Time of attack) was at 7.30 am. The company was divided into two halves. The first half company (attack) in rear to assaulting Battns & the rear half company (reserve) in rear of the supporting battns. A number of casualties occurred in no-man's land — 2/Lt WATSON & CALLAGHAN being killed & 2/Lt DONNELL being wounded. During the advance of the M.G. Coy it was seen that some of the troops which were beyond the left flank of the brigade were retiring. Consequently as many guns as could be got were put on that flank. 2/Lt SIMPSON was wounded (not running). M.G. Coy HQ was established in the DINGLE TRENCH at ROUND WOOD. The enemy kept up intense artillery fire throughout that day and night. 2/Lt MILLICAN was wounded that afternoon in but of CRUCIFIX TRENCH aft. Communication on that day was only established with seven guns, but firm	TRENCH MAP ONLERS to T/7/00
		8/9/16	other guns were known the somewhere in the front line.	
SUNKEN RD	2/7/16		The whole day passed comparatively peacefully. Supplies arrived in the evening	

T2131. Wt. W708—776 500000. 4/15. Sir J. C. & S.

WAR DIARY or INTELLIGENCE SUMMARY.

(Erase heading not required.)

Army Form C. 2118.

Place	Date	Hour	Summary of Events and Information	Remarks and references to Appendices
SUNKEN RD.	2/7/16		Communication was established with Bde HQ and news received to that effect. Bde wire ending thus — "Hearty Congratulations stout ranks". M.G.C. in the splendid way in which they brought up their guns yesterday. Nothing was head of the whereabouts of 2/Lt MUCKRIDGE, but it was later discovered that he had been killed; the conclusion is that he must have been killed on July 1st. All the guns in the line were assembled at H.Q., the total personnel which collected that evening numbered 45 including 2 Officers — Lt Cy & 2nd in Command, Lieut RICHARDSON.	
	July 3rd 1916		We arrived at our assembly trenches at 3 a.m. July 3rd. On reporting to Bde HQ the General stated that he had heard good things said of the M.G.C. on all sides.	Bde.
	3/7/16		The assembly trenches were met by 2/Lts CATCOLDHAMMAN F E TRANTER. In the early afternoon (after as great a clean up as possible) 6 guns were placed in position on SAUSAGE the trenches dir of SAUSAGE SUPPORT TRENCH in the protection of the Brigade Lt Flank.	

WAR DIARY
or
INTELLIGENCE SUMMARY.
(Erase heading not required.)

Army Form C. 2118.

Place	Date	Hour	Summary of Events and Information	Remarks and references to Appendices
ASSEMBLY TRENCHES S/1428/40&1 &4	3/7/16		It was just reported to the Brigade that they were in position, when news was received that the division was to be relieved. The 8 Suss. from SAUSAGE SUPPORT were recalled and all the scouts taken down to HAPPY VALLEY. The Scouts now numbered 15, including two damaged by shell & one that had been picked up from the German Trenches. When the Cheshires were ordered to lead the way to DERNANCOURT, the remaining Officer Cy had been leading 75 (2nd men hand forced up) lead the way to DERNANCOURT & arrived at 1am July 4th. M.H.C. — The names of those mentioned for good work were as follow:— 2/Lt G.H. COLDHAM. 5399 L/Cpl A HOVELL " H.C. MILLIGAN. 5406 Pte W. HIBBERT Lieut Adj. RICHARDSON. 5389 " T HARTLAND 8091 Sgt. W. MONEY 5402 " T OGDEN 8674 " V. FENNEMORE, 22115 " F. WILSON. 8101 Signaller S. BURGESS. M.H.C.	

Army Form 2118.

WAR DIARY
or
INTELLIGENCE SUMMARY.
(Erase heading not required.)

Instructions regarding War Diaries and Intelligence Summaries are contained in F.S. Regs., Part II. and the Staff Manual respectively. Title pages will be prepared in manuscript.

Place	Date	Hour	Summary of Events and Information	Remarks and references to Appendices
				Ref/map FRANCE 1:100 000 AMIENS.
DERNANCOURT	4/7/16	8am	Entrained. Transport moved by road under Bde Tpt Officer.	
AILLY-SUR-SOMME	"	1pm	Arrived and marched to YZEUX	
YZEUX	"	4pm	Arrived; transport arrived 4.30pm. All settled in billets at 6pm. Etc.	
"	5/7/16		Congratulatory address by G.O.C. 64th Inf Bde. Etc	
"	6/7/16		General clean up and in sputring all gun hit and him hit	
			Congratulatory address to whole brigade by G.O.C. 20th Division	
"	6/7/16	10.30pm	Arrival of 20 O.R's as reinforcements. Etc.	
"	7/7/16		2/Lts H.J. WOODINGTON and J.C. HOGG arrived as reinforcements	
"	"	12.0pm	Coy moved to FOUR DRINOY.	
FOUR DRINOY	"	5pm	" arrived and billeted. G.O.C.	
"	9/7/16	3pm	Transport moved under Bde Tpt Officer. (Destination VILLE) Bivouac	
			night 9 – 10/7/16 at QUERRIEU. Etc	
"	10/7/16	12.30pm	Company starts on march to entrain at AILLY-SUR-SOMME.	
BREVILLY	"	2pm	Arrived and waited till 9.30pm	
AILLY-SUR-SOMME	"	11pm	Arrived at the station and waited till 1am 11/7/16. Etc.	
			Transport arrived in VILLE at 11pm.	

Army Form C. 2118.

WAR DIARY
or
INTELLIGENCE SUMMARY.
(Erase heading not required.)

Instructions regarding War Diaries and Intelligence Summaries are contained in F. S. Regs., Part II. and the Staff Manual respectively. Title pages will be prepared in manuscript.

Place	Date	Hour	Summary of Events and Information	Remarks and references to Appendices
MILLY-SUR-SOMME	11/7/16	1am	Entrained and began journey to CORBIE at 2am.	
CORBIE	"		8am Coy arrived and marched to VILLE	
VILLE	"	8am	" and was billeted	Etc.
"	12/7/16	6pm	Coy marched out to take up position in support	
			Transport parked W of MEAULTE.	
			Two guns were put in QUADRANGLE SUPPORT, Two in QUADRANGLE TRENCH and two along the Northern edge of BOTTOM WOOD and two in reserve in a trench at FRICOURT.	
BOTTOM WOOD			HQ was in a dug out in S-W corner of BOTTOM WOOD. Two positions were taken over from the 110th BRIGADE.	Etc.
	13/7/16		Position unchanged. 2/Lt Savoury Owens Casey for Hutchings up of lines 2/Lt A STANLEY arrived.	
	13/7/16		In the evening of the 13th July the 8 guns were concentrated in the EASTERN END of QUADRANGLE SUPPORT TRENCH	Etc.
	14/7/16		Position unchanged. We were here in close support of the 110th Brigade, who at 3.25 am made their successful attack against the German second line position immediately N of MAMETZ WOOD.	Etc.

T2134. Wt. W708—776. 500000. 4/15. Sir J. C. & S.

WAR DIARY or INTELLIGENCE SUMMARY.

Army Form 2118.

Place	Date	Hour	Summary of Events and Information	Remarks and references to Appendices
	14/7/16		This [day?] secured, establishing their line along the western edge and western edge of BAZENTIN-LE-PETIT WOOD and the northern end of BAZENTIN-LE-PETIT village.	
	15/7/16		In the early hours he was never to take up position in this line. At 9am, orders were received to send 4 guns to the 10th K.O.Y.L.I., others with them to press to a position overlooking N.W. of BAZENTIN-LE-PETIT Village. The purpose of this was to fill the left flank of the 33rd Division and close any gap between the 31st & 33rd Divisions, both of whom were attacking enemy positions. Whilst moving through BAZENTIN-LE-PETIT village it was reported by 2/Lt F.E. TRANTER that the party, consisting of 10th R.O.Y. L.I. & the 4 guns of this Company, were seen by the enemy & shelled, with the result that we suffered 11 casualties, including 2/Lt H.T. WOODINGTON who was wounded. This party eventually, which south of the village. About 8 p.m. we received orders to take up positions we held the previous night. This was therefore done.	MAP MONTAUBAN 1/20,000

WAR DIARY or INTELLIGENCE SUMMARY

Army Form 2118.

Place	Date	Hour	Summary of Events and Information	Remarks and references to Appendices
BAZENTIN-LE-PETIT WOOD	16/7/16		The day passed quietly. In the evening orders were received to relieve the 110th Bde in BAZENTIN-LE-PETIT WOOD & village after the distribution of rations. The guns were therefore ordered to advance along the Railway running through MAMETZ WOOD to BAZENTIN-LE-PETIT. The relief was complete by about 9 p.m. This consisted of 2 guns S. Western side of BAZENTIN-LE-PETIT WOOD, 2 guns on the N western side of the wood, 2 guns No them side of the wood close to the village. That night orders were received from the General for a Gun to be placed at the southern edge of the village. This was completed by midnight.	
	17/7/16		The Horses remain in[?] Guns were kept in reserve in VILLA TRENCH. Instructions having been received to place it reserve guns in FOREST TRENCH, this trench was reconnoitred & suitable positions selected. About 10 am these guns & gun teams were taken up into readiness in VILLA TRENCH. They were in the point of starting when a German 5.9 shell landed right in the trench, & as a result we had 10 casualties including 3 killed, 1 died of wounds & 6 wounded.	

WAR DIARY
or
INTELLIGENCE SUMMARY.
(Erase heading not required.)

Army Form 2118.

Place	Date	Hour	Summary of Events and Information	Remarks and references to Appendices
AILLY-SUR-	23/7/16	4 pm	Transport moved off to entrain at LONGEAU.	
SOMME.		6 am	Coy " " "	
LONGEAU		7.15am	Transport arrived	
		8 am	" began to entrain	
		8.30 am	Coy arrived and began to entrain.	
ST POL	"	4 pm	Company detrained and began march to BERLENCOURT.	Ry/map FRANCE
BERLENCOURT	"	9.30 pm	" arrived and billeted. All ranks (B/Bn) in billets at 10.30 p.m.	57C-50B LENS.
"	24/7/16		Parades and general "smartening up" began, including physical drill, infantry drill, gas drill; instruction in intercom and topography.	g.a.r.
"	25/7/16		Coy had hot baths and complete change of underclothing.	g.a.r.
"	26/7/16		2/Lt J.L. SPENCE and 2/Lt G.I. WOODHAM – SMITH reported for duty as reinforcements and were taken on Coy strength accordingly.	g.a.r.
"	27/7/16		O.C. Coy made a tour of the trenches which No "C" Bn was to take over. Preparations begun for occupation of trenches.	g.a.r.
"	28/7/16	8 am	Transport moved to WANQUETIN under Tpt Officer.	
"		11 am	Coy moved in motor Busses to WANQUETIN and arrived 1 pm.	

Army Form C. 2118.

WAR DIARY
or
INTELLIGENCE SUMMARY.
(Erase heading not required.)

Instructions regarding War Diaries and Intelligence Summaries are contained in F.S. Regs., Part II and the Staff Manual respectively. Title pages will be prepared in manuscript.

Place	Date	Hour	Summary of Events and Information	Remarks and references to Appendices
WANQUETIN	29/7/16	7.30pm	Coy with Transport moved to ARRAS. Traffic was very congested and very much delayed the march of the Brigade.	
ARRAS	"	11.65pm	Arrived at billets. All material unloaded and limbered wagons returned to DUISANS. Transport arrived at DUISANS at 3.30 am 29/7/16. Got	
DUISANS	29/7/16	afternoon	Tpt parks with remainder of Bde Transport. The Quartermasters Stores is also established at this village.	O.K.
ARRAS		9 am	Company began to establish reliefs 41st M.G. Coy in the trenches. The trenches were very full of troops with the result that its completion of the relief was much delayed and not complete until 5½pm.	
			Arrangements for Rations Rations are dumped by A.S.C Supply Column at Q.M Stores at DUISANS, where they are made up into amounts for each Gun team & sent to Coy Hq in ARRAS at nights in lorries. There a permanent fatigue party from 9th K.R.R.L.I carry them to the cubbies dug into where they are delivered to the Gun teams.	

T2134. Wt. W708—776. 500000. 4/15. Sir J.C. & S.

WAR DIARY
INTELLIGENCE SUMMARY

Army Form C. 2118.

Place	Date	Hour	Summary of Events and Information	Remarks and references to Appendices
ARRAS	29/7/16		Passes etc. Requisition for rations may cease to be sent in daily during the day signed by the Cucan asking Officer. Infantry may cease to send them without a pass similarly signed. Stopping time is 9.30 – 10.30 pm. Etc.	
"	30/7/16		Guns inspected by OC Coy. The enemy is likely known gas in this part of the line and particular attention has to be paid to securing & keeping in repair the requisite protection against it. Difficulty is being experienced in obtaining PH & PHG Helmets, of which no pre war was issued before July 1st. It is our intention to obtain any, although circuits have been submitted. Etc.	
"	31/7/16		Quietness prevails on the front.	

A. E. Sevan Capt
OC 64 M.G. Coy.

WAR DIARY
or
INTELLIGENCE SUMMARY.
(Erase heading not required.)

Place	Date	Hour	Summary of Events and Information	Remarks and references to Appendices
	17/7/16		That same morning instructions were received from the General to place the two Coys, which were in the S-Western sist afterwards, in the position in some ???? pits, which had up till then been held by German snipers. This was to be done as soon as the position had been reoccupied by our own troops. These Coys were therefore taken from their positions and as soon as our infantry had occupied (?rifle pits) which were about 200 yds N. of BAZENTIN-LE-PETIT WOOD they were put in to position there. The enemy shelled us throughout that day & night. During the night we experienced some of this Gas shells. At about 1030 p.m. orders came through for our relief. Etc.	

Date	Hour	Summary of Events and Information	Remarks and references to appendices
1/7/16		Casualties in Action. Officers 7/u G.E. MOCKRIDGE, 7/u S.M. WATSON, 2/u TPA CALLAGHAN killed. 7/u G.A. SIMPSON, 7/u H.C. MILLIGAN D 7/u H.S.C. DONNELL wounded. O.Rs killed 16, wounded 34, shell shock 2, injured 1, died of wounds 1/ Gr. missing (believed killed) 1, missing 13 Total (all ranks) 72.	
		Awards Under authority grants by H.M. The King, Europe Commander awards Military Medals to 8091 Sgt Money. W. 8764 " Fanning. T dated 23/7/16. R.Br. 5272 Pte Stobart. W	

Fourth Army No. 266 (G).

21st Division.

Owing to the difficulty of assembling the Division it will not be possible for me to address them personally as I had wished.

I desire, therefore, that my congratulations and thanks may be conveyed to each Officer, N.C.O., and man of the Division for their excellent work and great gallantry during the Battle of the SOMME.

Their two successful assaults against the carefully prepared defences of the enemy's first and second systems is a feat of arms which will rank high in the attainments of the British Army.

No troops could have answered to the call of duty with greater dash, and the valour of the infantry, coupled with the excellent support afforded by the artillery, is deserving of the highest praise.

Your Corps Commander has repeatedly expressed to me his satisfaction both with the training of the Division before the first assault, and the behaviour of all ranks when in close contact with the enemy.

I regret that the 21st Division is leaving the Fourth Army, but they performed their part in this great battle in a manner that has filled me with admiration, and I trust that at some future time I may again have the honour of finding them under my command.

H. Rawlinson
General,
Commanding Fourth Army.

H.Q. Fourth Army.
21st July, 1916.

64th Brigade.

21st Division.

64th BRIGADE MACHINE GUN COMPANY

AUGUST ~~30~~ 1916

WAR DIARY or INTELLIGENCE SUMMARY

Army Form C. 118.

Place	Date	Hour	Summary of Events and Information	Remarks and references to Appendices
ARRAS	2/5/16		2/Lr O.C. CLUTTERBUCK reported for duty and was taken on the strength. This Officer is based in Transport Duties and took on the Transport. G.H.C.	
"	4/9/16		32 Reinforcements arrived. G.H.C.	
"	5/9/16		The enemy had been quiet to this date, but at 11.30 p.m. he opened an intensive bombardment on our front to support fires for 15 minutes, and attempted a raid which was beaten back. G.H.C.	
"	6/9/16		15 O.R.s in reinforcements arrived being transferred from 62 M.G. Coy. Coy still short of N.C.O.s. It was found in taking on this front of the line from the 41st M.G. Coy that considerable alterations in the gun positions were required, and the first days of this month have been devoted to executing these. G.H.C.	
"	9/9/16		The Germans make it a daily practice to shell ARRAS, and the shells generally fall in the Cathedral. G.H.C.	
"	10/9/16		20 Reinforcements arrived including 6 Sgts and 7 corporals, 2 signallers ? rangetakers. Strength of Company is now 170. Rations and now being taken up to ROCLINCOURT by Transport. G.H.C.	

WAR DIARY or INTELLIGENCE SUMMARY

Army Form C. 2118.

(Erase heading not required.)

Place	Date	Hour	Summary of Events and Information	Remarks and references to Appendices
ARRAS	13/8/16		2 men per gun team were relieved and all the N.C.O's. There are thus Lce. Sgts. & 4 Cpls. in the trenches and a similar number in rest. 3. O.R.s wounded by shell fire. 2/Lt A SHANLEY proceeded on a course of M.G. Instruction at CAMIERS with 2 other N.C.O's. G/W.	
"	16/8/16		2/Lt G.H. WHITAKER arrived and was taken on the strength. Rain has made the trenches very wet — their trenches retain water very easily and require much preparation for the winter months. G/W.	
"	17/8/16		C.O. proceeded on special leave, 2nd Lt A.W. RICHARDSON commands in his absence. G/W.	
"	18/8/16		Difficulty is being experienced in obtaining spare parts for the guns: up to the present a considerable number lost to knowns whereabouts during the period 12th – 17th July have not yet been replaced. G/W.	
"	20/9/16		2 men per gun team were relieved. This is how the regular practice — the men getting 2 weeks in the trenches and one week's rest. 4 Sgts. & 4 Cpls. take alternate weeks within the trenches.	

WAR DIARY
or
INTELLIGENCE SUMMARY

(Erase heading not required.)

Army Form C 2118.

Place	Date	Hour	Summary of Events and Information	Remarks and references to Appendices
ARRAS	20/9/16		The increase in the amount of machine gun ammunition to be drawn from A.O.D. is approved of, highly approved. GOC	
"	22/9/16		A violent artillery bombardment by us was perpetrated on the enemy about 9 p.m. after a continual firing throughout the day. This was an objective reply to a raid by a battn. of Leicester Regt. on enemy trenches. 1 OR joined the Company.	
"	23/9/16		Two guns in THELUS REDOUBT were replaced by guns from the 18th M.M.C. Battery; M.G. on Spurs has been placed in OBSERVATORY REDOUBT, and the other brought back into reserve. GOC	
"	27/8/16		C.O. returned and took over command of Coy.	
	30/9/16 9 p.m.		The guns of the 18th M.M. Gun Battery were in THELUS REDOUBT were known decided not to hold the M.G.S. 1 position (THELUS RIGHT) relieved. It was previously occupying that emplacement has been any more; the gun previously occupying that emplacement has been moved to a position in OBSERVATORY REDOUBT. 1 gun of this Coy relieves the 18 M.M.G. Battery's gun in M.G.S. 2 (THELUS LEFT) position. ["M.G.S. 4" means the 4th Vickers Machine Gun in its support line numbering from right to left; "M.G. 4" means the 4th Vickers M.G. in a Coy (which its front line) GOC]	

WAR DIARY
or
INTELLIGENCE SUMMARY

Army Form C. 2118.

Place	Date	Hour	Summary of Events and Information	Remarks and references to Appendices
ARRAS.	31/8/16		3 Other Ranks joined the Company.	
			A mine enterprise was attempted during the night. In the afternoon the artillery & trench mortars cut wire in front of 107↓ Trench. An innovation party went out in a forward sap after dark to wait for a German wiring party to appear. When that happened the party was to communicate with the F.O.O. and battalion were to open fire on the enemy, and at the same time a Lewis Gun & m.g. of the guns of the Company were also to fire. The Germans did not send a wiring party, but raided our trenches held by the 10th K.O.Y.L.I. A certain amount of damage was done and some of our men are reported missing. 33 casualties in all are reported.	
			Orders have been received to be prepared to move on Sept. 4th for "training in view of hard work in the near future".	

A.P.Kerin Capt.
O.C. 6th Northn. Div. Cy.

64th Brigade

21st Division.

64th BRIGADE MACHINE GUN COMPANY

SEPTEMBER 1 9 1 6

21/vol 7

ORIGINAL
WAR DIARY

64th MACHINE GUN COMPANY.

From 1st Sept. 1916 to 27th Sept. 1916.

Army Form C. 2118.

WAR DIARY
or
INTELLIGENCE SUMMARY.
(Erase heading not required.)

64th Coy. M.G. CORPS.

Instructions regarding War Diaries and Intelligence Summaries are contained in F.S. Regs., Part II and the Staff Manual respectively. Title pages will be prepared in manuscript.

Place	Date	Hour	Summary of Events and Information	Remarks and references to Appendices
ARRAS	1/9/16		1 OR wounded. Strength unchanged. Off. strength g.o.c.	Ref map LENS. 1/100000
"	2/9/16		1 OR " and strength of the strength. 1 OR taken on strength	
			3 ORs struck off strength from date 1/9/16, 16/9/16 and 26/9/16 returned from h.c. course at CAMIERS.	
			1/m A SHAWLEY struck and 2 ORs returned from h.c. course at CAMIERS.	
			Strength off. 1 OR returned from a course of training. Off. strength g.o.c.	
"	3/9/16	10 a.m.	OT. 106 M.G. Cy arrived and proceeded to take over 2 of this Coy's guns & 6 N.C.Os were employed round the positions.	
"	"	11.30 p.m.	Relief began two hours late. The relieving Coy sent 3 guns & teams to the wrong dump.	
"	"	2 p.m.	Transport that was not required to hire material from the lorries proceeded to IZEL-LES-HAMEAU. (Ref map LENS 1/100000) g.o.c.	
DUISANS	4/9/16	7 a.m.	Arrival of the rest party at DUISANS where breakfast was taken.	
		8.30 a.m.	Company + T.M Batty moved off to IZEL-LES-HAMEAU	
IZEL-LES-HAMEAU		noon	Arrived & found that billets were difficult to obtain owing to the presence of the R.F.C 9 2 other Battys	
		7 p.m.	All arrangements were complete. Orders were received that	

T2134. Wt. W708—77Œ 500000. 4/15. Sir J. C. & S.

WAR DIARY or INTELLIGENCE SUMMARY

Army Form C.118

Place	Date	Hour	Summary of Events and Information	Remarks and references to Appendices
TILLOY- LES- HAMEAU	4/9/16		had training was the indulged in with plenty of marching. It was shortly found that many men were out of training after 5 or 6 weeks in the trenches.	
"	6/9/16		1 OR went to attend H.Q. Course of Instruction at H.Q. Capt. Ross Dept. G.O.C. Sections were allotted to officers as follows No 1 {2/Lt GUDGHAM / 2/Lt J.T. HOGGS No 2 {2/Lt J.T. HOGGS / or CUTHERBUCK No 3 {1/Lt J.L. SPENCE / 2/Lt F.E. TRANTER No 4 {2/Lt A.M. RICHARDSON / 2/Lt A. SHANLEY The usual H.Q. Training was carried on.	
	8/9/16		2 ORs taken on the strength - Reinforcements. G.O.C. Open warfare practised. Lecture by G.O.C. 64 INF. BDE. The news that we are going back to the SOMME given out. Such demonstration.	
			1 OR taken on strength (7/9/16).	
	10/9/16		2 ORs & 10th R. Oy. LT atta for training returned to their Battn. Orders by G.O.C. 21st Division. That about our coming return to the Battle of the SOMME, and an appeal to uphold its name of the division & finally "hall mark" its achievements during the period July 1st-18th.	

T2134. Wt. W708—770. 500000. 4/15. Sir J.C. & S.

WAR DIARY or INTELLIGENCE SUMMARY

Army Form C.118.

Place	Date	Hour	Summary of Events and Information	Remarks and references to Appendices
IZEL-LES- HAMEAU	10/9/16		Inspection of Transport by G.O.C. 64 INF BDE. The Service Company formally upon the turn out. Ott.	
"	11/9/16		hired to CANETTEMONT preparatory to entraining. Arrived at 7 p.m. Orders received at 11 p.m. to send transport, minus 3 Limber wagons and Cooks Cart and Officers horses, to meet rest of Bn. Tpt at Cros Rds. immediately N. of the 1st E in REBREUVIETTE. They are to billet at SARTON (night 11/12th inst.) Company and remaining transport are to return at 3.30 am 13th inst at FREVENT and start for HEILY (Ref ATTIENS map 1/100000) on arrival to march to DERNANCOURT where the Staff Cap! will meet it. Ott. Transport couplied into other values.	Ott AMR
CANETTEMONT	12/9/16			
DERNANCOURT	13/9/16		Company entrained at FREVENT and detrained at HEILY marched to DERNANCOURT where they bivouacked	AMR
"	14/9/16		Company remained at DERNANCOURT	AMR
FRICOURT CAMP.	15/9/16	6 am	Company marched to FRICOURT CAMP (O.O. 75. dd. 14/9/16). At 3.15 pm moved to POMMIERS REDOUBT CAMP.	AMR

WAR DIARY or INTELLIGENCE SUMMARY.

Army Form C. 2118.

Place	Date	Hour	Summary of Events and Information	Remarks and references to Appendices
POMMIERS REDT.	16/9/16	2.30 a.m	Coy. marched into action near FLERS, and took part in attack by Bde. on FLEA Trench, N.E. FLERS. No.1 Section took up positions about 70* N. of FLEA Trench. No.2 Sect. in FLEA Trench, No.3 Sect in FLERS Trench, No.4 about 100* S. of SWITCH Trench. A fair amount of firing was done at odd parties of the enemy. Two M.G.S. and one Sniper were located. At dusk No.4 Sect. took up positions on left of No.2 Sect.	a.u.R.
FLERS	17/9/16	2 a.m	Preparations were made to withstand a counter-attack wh. never developed. From 9 am till dusk enemy shelled us very heavily. 2/Lt. and A/Capt.	
		2.30 p.m	G. H. COLDHAM was severely wounded in the head and left leg. O.C. 165th Coy was arranging for relief during afternoon. Casualties Offs. 1. 2/Lt G H COLDHAM O.Rs. 1 killed 6 wounded 1 missing. Company relieved at midnight. Returned to POMMIERS CAMP. At 3.15 p.m. marched back to FRICOURT CAMP.	a.u.R
POMMIERS CAMP	18/9/16		Company rested	a.u.R
FRICOURT CAMP	19/9/16		Company rested	a.u.R
"	20/9/16	11 am	Brigade addressed Bde.	a.u.R
"	21/9/16		Company rested. Capt. A.E. Bevan handed over the Command of the Coy. to Lt. A.N. RICHARDSON, the 2nd-in-C., in consequence of illness.	a.u.R

Army Form C. 2118.

WAR DIARY
or
INTELLIGENCE SUMMARY.
(Erase heading not required.)

Instructions regarding War Diaries and Intelligence Summaries are contained in F. S. Regs., Part II and the Staff Manual respectively. Title pages will be prepared in manuscript.

Place	Date	Hour	Summary of Events and Information	Remarks and references to Appendices
	1916			
FRICOURT CAMP	22/9	9.30 a.m.	Left FRICOURT CAMP for POMMIERS REDOUBT CAMP, which we left at 3.30 p.m. At 5 p.m. we reached H.Q. 62nd Infy. Bde. and arranged for the relief of 62nd M.G. Co. in the line to the right of GUEDECOURT. Sections 1, 2, & 3 went in. Sect. 4 remained at H.Q., N. of BERNAFAY WOOD.	AnR REF. MAP. ALBERT Sheet Combined 1/40,000 AnR
BERNAFAY WOOD	23/9		Company was in line	
"	24/9	7 pm	Company moved into battle positions, Sects. 3 & 4 in FRONT LINE, Sects 1 & 2 in Support.	
GUEDECOURT	25/9	10 am	H.Q. moved with Bde. H.Q. to 1000 yds S. of FIERS. At 12.30 pm Bde attacked but made no progress. 2/Lt. B. SHANLEY was killed and 2/Lt. G.H. WHITAKER wounded. 5 a.m. H.Q. moved up to FRONT LINE.	AnR
"	26/9	6 am.	Bde. advanced and reached its objective. Coy took up positions in accordance. 10 guns in FORWARD LINE, 2 guns in GIRD TRENCH, 4 guns in RESERVE. M.Gs had several excellent targets, notably enemy retiring from GUEDECOURT, and did great execution. 2/Lts F.E TRANTER and J.C. HOGG were instrumental in capturing 360 prisoners. 2/Lt F.E.TRANTER was slightly wounded. Casualties killed: the officer, 7 O.Rs.	
		11.30 pm	Wounded two Officers 22 O.Rs. Coy relieved by 62 M.G. Co.	AnR

An Richardson Lt

Army Form C.2118.

WAR DIARY
of
INTELLIGENCE SUMMARY.

Place	Date	Hour	Summary of Events and Information	Remarks and references to Appendices
BERNAVES	27/9			
	27/9		Coy Rested. Capt. P.C. BIRD arrived from 153 M.G.Coy to take command. 2/Lts J.H. HERBERTSON and R.E. MAY joined the Coy. 28 O.Rs were sent to support 110 M.G.Coy.	AWL
	28/9		Coy Rested	AWL
	29/9		do	AWL
	30/9		do	AWL
RIBEMONT	1/10 1 am		Coy moved to bivouacs at RIBEMONT. Reached bivouacs at 8 pm. New men put each one hour. Coy rested. 2/Lt. J.K. HALL reported.	AWL
	2/10		Entrained for new area. Reached LONGPRÉ 6 pm. Marched to MONFLIERS, in comfortable billets	ABBEVILLE 1/100,000.
MONFLIERS	3/10			
	4/10		Lt G.F. MASON reported. Coy rested and reorganized 2 6 O.Rs attached to 110 Bn since 28/9/16 rejoined. No casualties.	
	5/10		Entrained at ABBEVILLE for a new area.	
	6/10		Arrived at CHOCQUES. Marched to BURBURE. In comfortable billets	
BURBURE	7/10 to 9/10		Coy training. 7092 Sgt. F.A. EASON and 10709 Pte. J. PICKETT awarded the Military Medal for gallantry in action during 25/26 Sept.	HAZEBROUCK 1/100,000
	10/10		Coy La Med at AUCHEL.	AWL

Vol 8

War Diary
of
6th M.G. Co.
for
month of October, /16.

Army Form C. 2118.

WAR DIARY
or
INTELLIGENCE SUMMARY.
(Erase heading not required.)

Instructions regarding War Diaries and Intelligence Summaries are contained in F. S. Regs., Part II. and the Staff Manual respectively. Title pages will be prepared in manuscript.

Place	Date	Hour	Summary of Events and Information	Remarks and references to Appendices
BURBURE	11/10	7.30 am	Coy marched to BETHUNE, and billeted. A conference with G.O.C. Bde was held in the afternoon by the lessons from recent fighting, attended by Capt. BIRD and LT. A.N. RICHARDSON. LT. N.F. DIXON reported as 2nd-in-Command.	
BETHUNE	12/10		C.O. and 2.in-C. visited the trenches round CAMBRIN to arrange for relief from 97th M.G.Co. At night all M.G. material was dumped at WHITE HOUSE	MAP. 36C. A.20.c.3.3.
"	13/10		Coy marched to CAMBRIN and began relief at 10.45 am. Relief was complete at 4 pm. Very little information re the line could be elicited from 97 M.G.Coy, and several guns were wrongly marked on the map. The dispositions taken over were FRONT LINE 3 guns (No 1 Sect) SUPPORT LINE 6 guns, RAILWAY KEEP 2 guns, ARTHURS g KEEP 1 gun, in Reserve in ANNEQUIN one Sect (No 2). Advanced H.Q. (C.O. & C.S.M.) in FACTORY TRENCH. REAR H.Q. ANNEQUIN. NIGHT firing (about 2000 2ds) took place.	
	14/10 16/10		LT. A.N. RICHARDSON left to take Command of the 164th M.G.Co. A/Sgt WRIGHT went down to the BASE being under age.	ANR
CAMBRIN	17/10		REAR H.Q. was shifted from ANNEQUIN to Ate Mayors Grounds CAMBRIN near TOURBIÈRES REDOUBT.	

WAR DIARY
or
INTELLIGENCE SUMMARY.
(Erase heading not required.)

Army Form C.118.

Instructions regarding War Diaries and Intelligence Summaries are contained in F. S. Regs., Part II. and the Staff Manual respectively. Title pages will be prepared in manuscript.

Place	Date	Hour	Summary of Events and Information	Remarks and references to Appendices
CAMBRIN	19/10		Advanced Coy HQ moved back to REAR COY HQ CAMBRIN from FACTORY TRENCH.	1A
"	20/10		Two guns in the FIRING LINE were moved out to SUPPORT LINE by order of the Brigade Commander. 9,000 ROUNDS were fired during the night on selected TARGETS behind enemies line.	1A
"	24/10		2/Lt TRANTOR sent on leave. Has been since posted to report to Commandant BASE DEPOT GRANTHAM.	1A
"	27/10		Harassing night firing carried out 9,600 rounds fired.	1A
"	29/10		M.G. BARRAGE SCHEME worked out from 3 guns in VILLAGE LINE RANGE for firing about 1600 yds elevation between 2° and 3°.	1A

T2134. Wt. W708—776. 500000. 4/15. Sir J. C. & S.

CONFIDENTIAL

Vol 9

WAR DIARY

- OF -

64 M.G. Coy.

from 1st Nov. to 30th Nov/16

WAR DIARY
INTELLIGENCE SUMMARY

Army Form C.2118.

(Erase heading not required.)

Place	Date	Hour	Summary of Events and Information	Remarks and references to Appendices
CAMBRIN.	4/11/16		One gun in the front line was moved back to Coel Posts Trench by order of the Brigadier Commander. No guns (Vickers) were kept in front. The Brigade front was given on a level gun in Shaft Head the same at and aiming Mark the Shaft Head of the guns at forms of Teken. Thus enabling guns to fire on distant targets with greater accuracy for whilst stick was just put in front to muzzle the line was zero. Able operations in which we made a turning raid on the enemies lines. 5 guns firing overhead BARRAGE on the enemies back lines fired in 5 minutes 6,500 rounds.	
"	6/11/16		After one was laid on the VILLAGE LINE from H.Q. CAMBRIN, to enable messages from BARRAGE FIRE from 3 guns in the line to reach the Officer in Charge of guns quickly.	N.T.H.
"	15/11/16			

WAR DIARY or INTELLIGENCE SUMMARY

Army Form C.2118.

Place	Date	Hour	Summary of Events and Information	Remarks and references to Appendices
CAMBRIN	28/9/16		Much useful work was done by V50. VILLAGE Emplacements along with the Divisional O.P. Gates. 19 German working parties were engaged successfully in the open. Emplacements and trenches were greatly improved by the use of sandbags and iron pickets. On an average during the month about 8,000 rounds were fired in overhead targets during the day and night. During the 28th Nov 1916 we were relieved by the 18th Coy M.G. Corps. 9 guns on the left by the Brigade front were handed over to the 71st Coy M.G.C.	N.74
BETHUNE	29/9/16		Marched back to Billets in BETHUNE. 1st Day's rest in BETHUNE.	

Vol 10

Confidential.

64 M.G.Co.

**War Diary
for
December, 1916.**

Army Form C. 2118.

WAR DIARY
or
INTELLIGENCE SUMMARY

(Erase heading not required.)

Instructions regarding War Diaries and Intelligence Summaries are contained in F. S. Regs., Part II and the Staff Manual respectively. Title Pages will be prepared in manuscript.

Place	Date	Hour	Summary of Events and Information	Remarks and references to Appendices
BETHUNE.	20/12/16 to 6/12/16		2nd LIEUT. G.E. TOLLER joined this Company on the 29/12/16 for duty from the M.G. Base Depot CAMIERS. LIEUT. J.C. HOGG proceeded on leave to U.K. G.O.C. 21st Division inspected Company Transport and remarked favourably about it.	PVB. PVB.
VERMELLES	11/12/16 to 27/12/16.		Relieved 110th Company in HOHENZOLLERN SECTOR. No casualties during tour of duty. Excellent emplacements and well placed. They could be improved a little by enlarging the loopholes. Overhead fire was carried out at an average of 6–7 thousand rounds being fired daily. Rather poor barrage scheme it being too much dependent on Brigades on flanks. Trenches rather wet — no guns in firing line. Fairly quiet on the whole.	PVB.
	27/12/16.		Marched to NOEUX LES MINES — poor billets — relieved by 16 Coy Machine Gun Corps.	PVB.
	28/12/16 to 31/12/16.		Started training, also football + boxing	PVB.

Percy C Bush Captain
Comdg 64th Company
Machine Gun Corps

WAR DIARY
or
INTELLIGENCE SUMMARY

Army Form C 2118.

64 M.G. Coy.

Vol XI

Place	Date	Hour	Summary of Events and Information	Remarks and references to Appendices
NOEUX LES MINES	1st to 18th		Coy Resting. Carried out numerous Tactical Schemes for attack and defence. Route march for the week commanded at Table of march for each Friday. Brigaded H.Q. each Friday. Turning attenuous afternoons to provide men turning over to 3 Lattice of Company Run.	
"	19th to 21st		Given over to Brigade Horse Show. Coy had some trouble in Pair of mules entered for clear and 1 Officers Scharger in class 5. Won 1st Prize for Mules. Range entry. Mulier and Pair of Mules.	
NOEUX LES MINES	22nd		Brigade Commanders inspected Coy on Transport Field. Turn out equipment of men excellent.	
"	23rd		Brigade Marathon Race. Run between 5 or 6 miles Coy obtained 9rd & 5th.	
			About 30 entries from Coy.	

Army Form C. 2118.

WAR DIARY
or
INTELLIGENCE SUMMARY
(Erase heading not required.)

Place	Date	Hour	Summary of Events and Information	Remarks and references to Appendices
NOEUX LES MINES	26th		Horses & men fit. Must range 30 paces between horses & mules. C.O. went round the lines & made arrangements for carrying out believe ate given in lieu of following day.	
"	27th		Sudden orders to move at once. Coy. left NOEUX LES MINES afternoon 28th January for CHOCQUES.	
CHOCQUES	28th		LEFT CHOCQUES by train for Mechanion destination.	
ESPUELBECK	29th		Detrained ESPUELBECK early in morning and marched to billets near LA MOTTE.	
LA MOTTE	31st		In billets near LA MOTTE.	

N.A. Dyson, Captain
O.C. 84th Coy. Machine Gun Corps.

WAR DIARY or INTELLIGENCE SUMMARY

64th Coy MG Corps
21st Grenvier

Vol/2

Place	Date	Hour	Summary of Events and information	Remarks and references to Appendices
LA MOTTE	9/2/17		Resting at LA MOTTE FARM.	
"	10/2/17		Left LA MOTTE and entrained at ESQUELBECK and CHOQUES. Detrained about 7-30 p.m. Marched to BETHUNE and stayed the night.	
BETHUNE.	11/2/17		Took over CAMBRIN SECTOR from 158th M.G. Coy. 14 Guns in line & Guns in reserve in ANNEQUIN.	
TRENCHES	21/2/17		18 Guns opened fire on the NORTHERN part of AUCHY-LES-LA BASSEE. Prisoners reports considerable casualties inflicted. Germans have been raiding test men must keep to their trenches in their front line.	
"			AUCHY.	
"	22/2/17		4 Guns in front line in support RAID. 2 on the night Stokes Pt RAID and 2 on ley of flanks RAID into Off. g	

WAR DIARY
or
INTELLIGENCE SUMMARY

Army Form C. 2118.

Place	Date	Hour	Summary of Events and Information	Remarks and references to Appendices
TRENCHES	30/5/17		Secret gun position at the top of Munster Parade trench taken over by one 13 Bng gun teams as a permanent position. 30 teams position on O'Brien nests during the night.	

M.J. Bryan Lieut. [signature]
Comdg. 65th Coy. Machine Gun Corps

Army Form C.2118.

WAR DIARY
or
INTELLIGENCE SUMMARY.
(Erase heading not required.)

6th th M. G. Coy

Vol 13

Place	Date	Hour	Summary of Events and Information	Remarks and references to Appendices
CAMBRIN.	1st		TRENCHES. Owing to rain in muddy condition.	M.7.*.
"	4th		TRENCHES. Relieved by the 15th Coy. M.G. Corps. Position at top Munster Parade Tunnel. Coy marched to Béthune and billeted for night.	M.7.*.
BÉTHUNE	5th		Marched to Robecq. Billeted in Robecq.	M.7.*.
ROBECQ.	6th		Billeted in Robecq.	M.7.*.
ROBECQ.	9th		Marched to Mazingham. Billeted in Mazingham.	M.7.*.
MAZINGHAM.	10th		Billeted in Mazingham.	M.7.*.
"	11th		Marched to Pressy-les-Pernes. Billeted for night.	M.7.*.
PRESSY-LES-PERNES.	12th		Marched to Framecourt. Billeted for night.	M.7.*.
FRAMECOURT.	13th		Marched to Brevillers. Billeted in Brevillers.	M.7.*.
BREVILLERS.	14th		Billeted in Brevillers.	M.7.*.
"	23rd		Marched to Grenas. Billeted in Grenas.	M.7.*.
GRENAS.	24th		Billeted in Grenas.	
"	27th		Marched to Berles-les-Bois. Billeted for night.	
BERLES-LES-BOIS.	28th		Marched to Bienvillers. Billeted in Bienvillers.	M.7.*.

Army Form C.118.

WAR DIARY
or
INTELLIGENCE SUMMARY.
(Erase heading not required.)

Instructions regarding War Diaries and Intelligence Summaries are contained in F. S. Regs., Part II. and the Staff Manual respectively. Title pages will be prepared in manuscript.

Place	Date	Hour	Summary of Events and Information	Remarks and references to Appendices
BIENVILLERS	30th		Marched to BOIRY ST MARTIN. Attached to 62nd Brigade.	Attached to G.O.C. M.38.

M.T. Dyson Lieut. for
Captain
Comdg. 64th Coy. Machine Gun Corps.

WAR DIARY
INTELLIGENCE SUMMARY

64th M.G. Coy

Army Form C. 2118.

Place	Date	Hour	Summary of Events and Information	Remarks and references to Appendices
BOIRY ST. MARTIN	APRIL 1.		No 2 Section under LIEUT HOGG was attached to 62nd Brigade for tactical reasons. The remaining 3 Sections were sent forward to the MONT ST. MARTIN - Ate HAMLENCOURT - BOISLEUX-AU-MONT railway line in support of the Infantry resistance along with the Infantry between the 3 two east named villages. Coy H.Q. remained at BOIRY ST MARTIN.	
	5.		2 Sections of the 110th M.G. Coy took over from my 3 Sections the defence of the above line. 62nd Brigade was relieved by 64th Brigade in the front trenches. No 2 Section again came under my command.	
	7.		My dispositions for the attack on this date was as follows. Lt BENNETT & 2/Lt RANKIN with 4 guns was attached to 1st East Yorks. Lt SPENCE with 2 guns	
	9.			

WAR DIARY
INTELLIGENCE SUMMARY
(Erase heading not required.)

Army Form C. 2118.

Place	Date	Hour	Summary of Events and Information	Remarks and references to Appendices
	April 9th		went out to number road MAP 51B S.W. T4 & 8.8. at midnight 8/9th in front of German HINDENBURG line near ST MARTIN SUR COTEUL the day revealed during the day the 9th and on our Battalions advancing past line on enemy wire. It is guns held about 60 to 70 yds in front jumping trench. We saw the enemy advancing the advance of our troops in many of them presented their front line towards and made for their support line thus affording there guns an excellent target which they quickly availed themselves of doing good execution. They were able also to assist the advance of the Infantry Lieut BENNETT's section which was attached to 1st East Yorks came into action in the German	

WAR DIARY
INTELLIGENCE SUMMARY
(Erase heading not required.)

Army Form C. 2118.

Place	Date	Hour	Summary of Events and Information	Remarks and references to Appendices
	APRIL			
	9th		Front line beating off a determined counter-attack about 6.30 P.M. 6 O/Rs casualties were 1 man killed 1 Officer & 3 men wounded.	
	10th		The enemy began counter-attacked with great violence and Sketchs the ground men during the previous day it was impossible to hold off the attack and the 4 gun teams were all casualties with the exception of 2/Lt Rankin and five other ranks. – Lieut BENNETT was killed fighting most gallantly with his section. Three demandes of my guns had not come into action the objective not being reached. The 110th Bde magazine covered my right flank. Casualties during this day were 1 Officer killed and 2 O.R. 13 O.R. missing.	

2353 Wt. W2514/1454 700,000 5/15 D. D. & L. A.D.S.S. Forms/C. 2118.

Army Form C. 2118.

WAR DIARY
INTELLIGENCE SUMMARY.
(Erase heading not required.)

Instructions regarding War Diaries and Intelligence Summaries are contained in F. S. Regs., Part II. and the Staff Manual respectively. Title pages will be prepared in manuscript.

Place	Date	Hour	Summary of Events and Information	Remarks and references to Appendices
	APRIL			
	11th		62nd Brigade relieved 64th Brigade in the line. Coy marched back to Boisleux St Marc. to rest.	
	19th		Marched to Blaireville. Billeted in this village for rest.	
	23rd		Marched to Mercatel arrived 5-30 P.M. Left this village for Boyelles at 2-30 A.M. on morning of 24th APRIL.	
	25th		Relieved 19th Coy M.G. Corps in line in front of ST MARTIN SUR COJEUL.	
	28th		2/Lieut RANKIN north R guns attached to 9th K.O.Y.L.I. Regt.	
	29th		Morning of this day 165 zolo of HINDENBERG line bombed down, and 4 guns attached to 9th K.O.Y.L.I. at T6 d R.7. Guns did not fire.	

WAR DIARY
or
INTELLIGENCE SUMMARY

Army Form C. 2118.

64th H.G. [?] Vol 15

Place	Date	Hour	Summary of Events and Information	Remarks and references to Appendices
HINDENBURG LINE	1/5/17		Coy. H.Q. on the HENIN-SUR-COJEUL - CROISILLES ROAD near HENIN.	NKH
	2/5/17		Coy. H.Q. moved up to HINDENBURG SUPPORT line Aug-out 21. Ref. Sheet 51b S.W. /30,000. 15th D.L.I. attacked down HINDENBURG line but were held up after reaching the German Battalion.	
	3/5/17		Block 4 guns were attached to the above Battalion for Tactical reasons under 2/Lieut HALL. 2 guns were Brigade and 2 in Reserve in a Sug-out. The Tanks attacked to the Brigade were unfortunately knocked out at the beginning of the operations. 10th K.O.Y.L.I. were in close support. 1st East Yorks Regt. in Brigade Reserve. 1 M.G. of the above Section was employed in enemy strong between the HINDENBURG FRONT and SUPPORT LINE during the attack. The attack was held up owing to the enemy's superior numbers and the failure of the tanks.	NKH
	4/5/17		Situation fairly quiet.	

WAR DIARY
or
INTELLIGENCE SUMMARY

(Erase heading not required.)

Army Form C.118.

Place	Date	Hour	Summary of Events and Information	Remarks and references to Appendices
HINDENBURG LINE	5/5/17		Advanced H.Q. moved back to its original place HENIN-SUR-COJEUL - CROISELLES. ROAD.	M.A.
—	8/5/17		Situation quiet. O.C. 62nd M.G. Coy took over command of 3 of my Sections in the line.	M.A.
—	9/5/17		O.C. Coy left for Rest Camp, BOULOGNE.	M.A.
—	11/5/17		The Coy less 3 Sections attached as above left for Rest Billets (BAILLEULVAL) arrived about	M.A.
BAILLEULVAL	12/5/17		3 P.M. Very good Billets. 3 Sections attached to O.C. 62nd M.G. Coy in the above village billeted with remainder of Coy.	M.A.
—	13/5/17		Training. Table mobile in Rest made lists for Tactical Scheme for Divisional M.G.O.	M.A.
—	24/5/17		C.M.G.O. fixed 25 Sections detailed for above. Rehearsed an attack of low lying ground near MONCHY.	M.A.
—	26/5/17		Inspected by Corps Commander.	M.A.

Army Form C. 2118.

WAR DIARY
or
INTELLIGENCE SUMMARY
(Erase heading not required.)

Instructions regarding War Diaries and Intelligence Summaries are contained in F. S. Regs., Part II. and the Staff Manual respectively. Title Pages will be prepared in manuscript.

Place	Date	Hour	Summary of Events and Information	Remarks and references to Appendices
BAILLEULVAL	30/5/17		Left BAILLEUVAL for Trenches at 2-30 P.M. Arrived BOYELLES and bivouaced the night. Took over in the trenches guns 10/98th Brigade.	N.A.
"	31/5/17		5. Guns in HINDENBURG LINE near FONTAINE-LES-CROISELLES, 3 guns in Support line and 4 guns in Reserve line. Coy. H.Q. in the BOIRY - BECQUERELLE - ST LEGER road near Jenner village.	N.A.

M.A. Ryan Lieut for.
O.C. 64th M.G. Coy

Army Form C. 2118.

WAR DIARY
or
INTELLIGENCE SUMMARY
(Erase heading not required.)

64th M.G. Coy. Vol 1/16

Place	Date	Hour	Summary of Events and Information	Remarks and references to Appendices
ST LEGER ~ BOIRY BECQUERELLE ROAD.	31st May to June 6		The Company relieved the 98th Machine Gun Company in the line. 16 Guns being at in Reserve at BOYELLES.	PUB
	JUNE 7th to JUNE 15th		Overhead fire schemes were carried out by the Section in Support from WALLER ROAD which runs due north from CROISILLES across the HINDENBURG LINE. The 4 Guns in support were instrumental in breaking up an Enemy air Barrage. The 4 Guns on our right made an attack. 6 Guns belonging to this Company were pushed forward into YORK TRENCH which runs about 500 yards N.W. of FONTAINE-LEZ-CROISILLES in a N.E direction. The Guns were so placed to form a Barrage firing on certain areas and suspected Enemy Machine Gun Emplacements. The attack however was held up, but the 6 Guns remained in YORK TRENCH in case of an Enemy counter-attack for 36 hours. During the attack 22,000 rounds were fired in half an hour by these Guns and it was reported that two Enemy Machine Guns had been knocked out by our fire, for as soon as the Barrage started the two M.G.s in question started to fire; however they were silenced immediately and were not heard in return again during the attack.	PUB
BOYELLES.	JUNE 19th		The Company was relieved by the 98th Company. The Company Entrained at 8 Echelon BOYELLES in the night of the 19/20th and at 5.30 am 20th marched to Rest billets at BIENVILLERS-AU-BOIS arriving there at 10 am. Excellent billets.	PUB
BIENVILLERS	JUNE 26th		A General Training Programme was carried out. The G.O.C. 64th Infantry Brigade inspected the Company. The turnout was excellent and the G.O.C. noted his appreciation of the fine condition of the transport.	PUB

2449 Wt. W14957/M90 750,000 1/16 J.B.C. & A. Forms/C.2118/12.

Army Form C. 2118.

WAR DIARY
or
INTELLIGENCE SUMMARY

(Erase heading not required.)

Instructions regarding War Diaries and Intelligence Summaries are contained in F. S. Regs., Part II and the Staff Manual respectively. Title Pages will be prepared in manuscript.

Place	Date	Hour	Summary of Events and Information	Remarks and references to Appendices
BERVILLERS.	June 29th		The Company marched to MOYENVILLE and took over "E" Camp from the 5th Machine Gun Company.	AB
MOYENVILLE.	June 30th		No 1 Section in reserve at C Lines.	PCB

Percy C Powel
Captain
Comdg. 64th Coy. Machine Gun Corps.

2449 Wt. W14957/M90 750,000 1/16 J.B.C. & A. Forms/C.2118/12.

Army Form C. 2118.

WAR DIARY
INTELLIGENCE SUMMARY
(Erase heading not required.)

4th Coy. M.G. Corps
Vol 17

Place	Date	Hour	Summary of Events and Information	Remarks and references to Appendices
MOYENVILLE – CROISILLES R^t SECTOR	1.7.17		The Company relieved the 100th Company, Machine Gun Corps in the Right Brigade Sector. Relief completed by 1 p.m. Company Headquarters was situated behind the railway at T.20.d.9.1. Disposition of Guns as follows. 4 Guns in the Front line, 4 in Support, 4 in Cruisilles line, and the remaining 4 Guns at Company Headquarters. During this tour the line was fairly quiet and no incidents of special moment occurred. The work of repairing and improving emplacements was continued. No Casualties occurred during this tour.	
	8.7.17		The Company was relieved by the 110th Company, Machine Gun Corps and marched back to MOYENVILLE, CAMP E, where the Company became Brigade Reserve.	PUB PUB
MOYENVILLE.			Gun Drill and Company Training was carried out during this rest. One Gun mounted to deal with hostile aircraft.	PUB
CROISILLES LEFT SECTOR	16.7.17		The Company relieved the 62nd Company, Machine Gun Corps in the Left Brigade Sector. Company Headquarters moved up to the TUNNEL. T.9.6.9.8. During this spell in the line. Overhead fire was carried out on tracks, Fontaine Wood and Canarios used by the enemy as Battalion H.Q^{rs}. Two new Emplacements were constructed at N.35.&.9.2. and T.5. a. 4.5.9.0. The distribution of the Guns was as follows. 4 Guns in front line, 2 in support and 6 Gun in Intermediate Support, the remaining 4 Guns at the transport at BOYELLES. During this spell in the line 3 men were wounded and 1 Gun put out of action by a piece of shrapnel.	PUB
MOYENVILLE.	24.7.17		The Company was relieved by the 62nd Company Machine Gun Corps and the Company became Brigade Reserve. Company and Gun Drill were carried out during this rest.	PUB PUB

Comdg. 4th Coy. Machine Gun Corps
Captain

Army Form C. 2118.

WAR DIARY
or
INTELLIGENCE SUMMARY
(Erase heading not required.)

64th Coy. M.G. Corps.
Vol /18

Place	Date	Hour	Summary of Events and Information	Remarks and references to Appendices
	1.8.17		The Company relieved the 110th Machine Gun Company in the RIGHT SECTOR, in front of FONTAINE. 3 Sections in the line and 1 at rest at Company Headquarters. The position of Company Headquarters was at T.21.d.9.1 (map 51B)	JKH
BULLECOURT 57 B S.W.4.	6.8.17		The 21st Division transferred to the VI Corps and the Company in consequence also transferred to the VI Corps. The dispositions of the Guns were as follows. The Company relieved the 19th Company Machine Gun Corps. 4 Gun front line - 4 Guns intermediate support and 4 in Reserve. 1 Section at Company Headquarters at T.30.c.3.9.	JKH
Do	19/20.		The S.O.S. signal (which was a rocket bursting into two Green & two White lights) went up from the H.Q.M.R. at U.27.3.d.7.5. at about 2am. The three defence Machine Guns opened fire at once and all S.O.S. Guns in that vicinity & those which covered same opened fire immediately. The Infantry reported that all Guns were firing clear of their parapet into No Man's Land and the manning of the parapet was quite unaffected in any way. The Major General congratulated the D.M.G.O. that the Machine Gunners concerned in the shoot and accurate barrage put down. In all an average of 1,000 rounds per Gun were fired. The effect of the barrage was not ascertainable as the ?shot and smoke of the Artillery Barrage made observation impossible.	JKH
MOYENVILLE	25.8.17		The rest of this tour was uneventful and the Company only had two casualties, two men being wounded. The Company (4ess 1 Section) was relieved by the 47th Company, Machine Gun Corps and marched to "B" Camp MOYENVILLE.	JKH
BOISLEU-AU-MONT	26.8.17		The Company marched to BOISLEUX-AU-MONT and stayed there until the 28th. The remaining Section which was still in the line rejoining.	JKH
Do	27.8.17		Captain P.C. BIRD ordered to report to M.G.T.C. Grantham. Lieut. Dixon appointed Captain & O.C Company vice LIEUT. J.K. HALL as 2nd in Command	JKH JKH

Army Form C.118.

WAR DIARY
or
INTELLIGENCE SUMMARY
(Erase heading not required.)

Instructions regarding War Diaries and Intelligence Summaries are contained in F. S. Regs., Part II. and the Staff Manual respectively. Title Pages will be prepared in manuscript.

Place	Date	Hour	Summary of Events and Information	Remarks and references to Appendices
BOULEU-AU-MONT.	29.8.17		The Company marched to the Rest Area at BERNECOURT. Good billets and the men comfortable. Training was carried out and special attention was given to Barrage Glances.	JH.
BERNECOURT.				

J.H.Hall for Captain
Cmdr. 84th Coy, Machine Gun Corps.

Army Form C 2118.

64 M.G. Coy

Vol 19

WAR DIARY
or
INTELLIGENCE SUMMARY.
(Erase heading not required.)

Instructions regarding War Diaries and Intelligence Summaries are contained in F.S. Regs., Part II. and the Staff Manual respectively. Title pages will be prepared in manuscript.

Place	Date	Hour	Summary of Events and Information	Remarks and references to Appendices
SCOTTISH WOOD	30/9/17	4 PM	The company arrived and were encamped here for the night 2/LIEUT RANKIN with 6 men & 6 R.E's went up to Battery position in the morning by the D.V.G.O & CAPTAIN DIXON. Selected in the future of clearing dugouts. The party took up SAA and formed a dump at GLENCORSE WOOD. They remained at the position till the night of 2/3rd October 1917	JW
	30/9/17	10 PM	Action of machine guns during the attack on the 4th October 1917 Dispositions of Guns were as follows. 4 Guns were attached to the 64th Infantry Brigade 8 Guns together with 8 guns from the 62nd Machine Gun Coy and 4 from the 287th M.G. Coy., formed a group under the command of Captain N.F. DIXON for Barrage fire. Guns were held in Reserve by D.M.G.O.	JW

Army Form C.2118.

WAR DIARY
or
INTELLIGENCE SUMMARY.
(Erase heading not required.)

 Wellington M.G. Coy Vol 20

Place	Date	Hour	Summary of Events and Information	Remarks and references to Appendices
SCOTTISH WOOD	30/9/17	4pm	The company arrived and were accomodated there for the night	
	30/9/17	10pm	2/Lt RANKIN. with 6 men & 6 R.E's went up to Battery positions selected in the morning by the D.M.G.O & Bower Decour. for the purpose of clearing dugouts. This party took out L.A.A. and formed a dump at GLENCORSE WOOD. They manned # at the positions till the night of 2/3rd Oct 1917.	J.K.H
			Action of machine Guns during the attack on the 4th Oct 1917. Dispositions of Guns were as follows. 4 Guns were attached to the 64th Infantry Brigade. 8 Guns together with 8 from the 63rd M.G Co. and 4 from Co. 237th M.G Co. formed a group under the Command of Captain W.F. Dixon for barrage fire.	J.K.H
			4 Guns were held in Reserve by the D.M.G.O	J.K.H

WAR DIARY
or
INTELLIGENCE SUMMARY.

Army Form C. 2118.

Place	Date	Hour	Summary of Events and Information	Remarks and references to Appendices
GLENCORSE WOOD	3/10/17	5PM	4 GUNS ATTACHED TO THE 64 INFANTRY BRIGADE. The section reported to the 15th D.L.I. It was under the command of 2/Lieut BUCKELL with 2/Lieut WHEELER as subsection officer. It was arranged that 2 guns were to go over with the right company under 2/Lieut BUCKELL and 2 with the left company under 2/Lieut WHEELER.	JRW
	3/10/17	8PM	2/Lieut WHEELER was buried with a shell and Sgt FLETCHER took charge.	JRW
	4/10/17	2.3AM	The section was then attached to the 10 ROYAL and moved forward with them to the assembly position and dug themselves in behind the infantry.	JRW JRW
	4/10/17	6AM	AT ZERO the guns advanced. Everything went well till they reached the edge of the wood J.10.C.58.10 when it was seen that the infantry were withdrawing. It was decided to stop the withdrawal & consolidate 2 guns were pushed out in front to give moral support. The infantry ranks since then seen advancing on the night.	JRW

2353 Wt. W3544/454 700,000 5/15 D. D. & L. A.D.S.S. Forms/C.2118.

WAR DIARY
or
INTELLIGENCE SUMMARY.

Army Form C.2118.

Place	Date	Hour	Summary of Events and Information	Remarks and references to Appendices
GLENCORSE WOOD MAP	30/9/17	5pm	GUNS ATTACHED to 64 INF.TH BRIGADE. The section reported to the 15 D.L.I. & was under the Command of 2/Lt BUCKELL with 2/Lt WHEELER as subsection Officer. It was arranged that 2 guns were to go out with the right company and under 2/Lt BUCKELL and 2 with the left company under 2/Lt WHEELER.	J.W.
"	3/10/17	8pm	2/Lt WHEELER was buried with a shell and Sergeant FLETCHER took charge.	J.W.
	4/10/17	2+3 am	The section was then attached to the 10 K.O.Y.L.I. & moved forward with them to the Assembly position. & dug themselves in behind the infantry.	J.W.
	4/10/17	6 am	At Zero- the guns advanced behind the infantry. Everything went well till they reached the edge of the wood J10 C58 10 which it was seen that the infantry were withdrawing. It was decided to stop the withdrawal & consolidate. 2 guns were pushed out in front to give moral support. Tanks were then seen advancing on the right, the infantry immediately formed up behind, and advanced with them	J.W.

WAR DIARY
or
INTELLIGENCE SUMMARY.
(Erase heading not required.)

Army Form C. 2118.

Place	Date	Hour	Summary of Events and Information	Remarks and references to Appendices
France			immediately formed up behind them and advanced with them. The advance was continued until the cross roads J.11.C.53.30, when word came round that the line would be held and consolidated. A gun was placed on the extreme right, the trench the East Yorks were holding. The only other gun that got up was placed practically on the cross roads.	
	4/10/17	3PM	The enemy were seen advancing towards the CHAT. BUK. on the right. The guns which were in the East Yorks trench, immediately opened fire and got good results.	JMcM
	7/10/17	11AM	The guns were relieved and came back to Transport lines (H.26.C.SHEET 28) 19 men & 2 nco's of the D.L.I. went over with the guns as carrying party.	JMcM
			ACTION OF BARRAGE GUNS.	
POLYGON	4/3 10-17	1AM	GUNS were placed in position during the nights of the 3rd & 3rd ammunition & Rations were carried up under the direction of 2/Lieut. JOHNSON (15 DLI) attached to us for carrying purposes. A party of 32 men & 2 nco's	Jay

Army Form C. 2118.

WAR DIARY
or
INTELLIGENCE SUMMARY.
(Erase heading not required.)

Instructions regarding War Diaries and Intelligence Summaries are contained in F. S. Regs., Part II. and the Staff Manual respectively. Title pages will be prepared in manuscript.

Place	Date	Hour	Summary of Events and Information	Remarks and references to Appendices
TRENCHES	4/10/17	2 AM	The guns were laid on their first Barrage Line. The position were heavily shelled from 3 AM.	JWF
		6-3 AM	At ZERO + 3 The guns open fire for 20 minutes when 2 guns were put out of action	JWF
		6·25	Guns were laid on second barrage and opened fire. Fire was continued till 7-30 when word was received (by runner) that objective had been taken. Guns ceased fire and were withdrawn by, laid on their S.O.S.	JWF
	4/10/17	11 AM	The O.C. 237 M.G. Coy made his headquarters with Captain DIXON	JWF
		3·30 AM	A shell landed in the door of the dugout (H.Q) killing the O.C. 237 M.G. Coy & 3 men, & wounded CAPTAIN DIXON,	JWF
		2/Lieut	PLEDGER and 5 men (CAPTAIN DIXON and SGT QUINTON have since died of wounds)	
	4/10/17	11 PM	Captain CHALMERS 62nd M.G. Coy. took command of the group. 4 guns were withdrawn and positions were re-organised.	JWF
	6/10/17	11 PM	The reserve action with reinforcements, manning 6 guns	JWF

Army Form C. 2118.

WAR DIARY
or
INTELLIGENCE SUMMARY.
(Erase heading not required.)

Place	Date	Hour	Summary of Events and Information	Remarks and references to Appendices
TRENCHES	7/10/17	12 MIDNIGHT	relieved The barrage guns which came back to Transport Lines. There six guns were withdrawn on the night of 7/8 October. The company then proceeded byrail to RENESCURE from the By road. Casualties during action were 1 OFFICER (DIED OF WOUNDS) 1 ORs (DIED OF WOUNDS) 4 ORs (KILLED) 2 OFFICERS WOUNDED & 14 other ranks.	

J.R. Hall
for O.C. 64 M.G.C.

Army Form C. 2118.

WAR DIARY
or
INTELLIGENCE SUMMARY.
(Erase heading not required.)

Instructions regarding War Diaries and Intelligence Summaries are contained in F. S. Regs., Part II. and the Staff Manual respectively. Title pages will be prepared in manuscript.

Place	Date	Hour	Summary of Events and Information	Remarks and references to Appendices
Trench	4/10/17	3pm	The advance was continued till the cross roads (J.11.c.53.30) when word came round that the line would be held & consolidated. A gun was placed on the extreme right, the trench the East Yorks were holding. The only other gun that got up was placed practically on the cross roads. The enemy were seen advancing towards the CHATEUX on the right, the gun which was on the East Yorks trench immediately opened fire and got good results.	JW
	7/10/17 on 11		These guns were relieved and came back to transport line (H25 C Sh28) 19 Men & 2 N.CO's of the D.L.I. went over with the guns as a carrying party	JW
			ACTION OF BARRAGE GUNS.	
POLYGON.	3 8/10/17	10am.	Guns were placed in Junction. During the nights of the 2nd + 3rd. ammunition & rations were carried up under the direction of 2/Lt JOHNSON. (15th D.L.I.) A party of 32 men & 2 N.CO's attached as for carrying purposes.	JW

2353 Wt. W2514/1454 700,000 5/15 D. D. & L. A.D.S.S. Forms/C 2118.

WAR DIARY
or
INTELLIGENCE SUMMARY.
(Erase heading not required.)

Army Form C. 2118.

D40

Place	Date	Hour	Summary of Events and Information	Remarks and
TRENCHES	4/10/17	2 am	The Germans were last on their first barrage line. The Germans were heavily shelled from 3 am.	
		6.3 am	At Zero + 3 the guns opened fire for 20 minutes when we were put out of action	
		6.25	Germs were laid on second barrage & thereafter fire. There was continued till 7.30 when word was received (by runner) that the objectives had been taken. Germs were immediately turned their S.O.S. lines.	JW
	4/10/17	11 am	The O.C. 237 M.G.C. made his H.Q. with Captain Dixon.	
		3.30 pm	A shell landed in the door of the dugout (H.Q.) killing the O.C. 237 M.G.C. & 3 men and wounding Captain Dixon, Lieut Pledger and 5 more. (Captain Dixon & Sgt Quirk since died of wounds)	JW
	4/10/17	11 pm	Captain CHALMERS. 62nd M.G.C. took command of the group. 4 guns were withdrawn and trackers were reorganized	JW
	5/10/17	11 pm	The Reserve section with reinforcements, manning 6 guns	JW

WAR DIARY
or
INTELLIGENCE SUMMARY.
(Erase heading not required.)

Army Form C. 2118.

Instructions regarding War Diaries and Intelligence Summaries are contained in F. S. Regs., Part II. and the Staff Manual respectively. Title pages will be prepared in manuscript.

Place	Date	Hour	Summary of Events and Information	Remarks and references to Appendices
TRENCHES	4/2/17	2 am	The Germans were last on their first barrage line. The trenches were heavily shelled from 3 am.	JRW
		6:3 am	At Zero + 3 the guns opfire for 20 minutes when 2 guns were put out of action	JRW
		6:25	Guns were last on word barrage & thence fire this was continued till 7.30 when word was received (by runner) that the objectives had been taken. Guns were immediately Lud on their S.O.S.	JRW
	5/2/17	11 am to 3.30	The O.C. 237 M.G.C. made his H.Q with Captain Dixon. A Shell landed in the door of the dugout (H.Q) Killing the O.C. 237 M.G.C. & 3 men and wounding Capt. Dixon, Lieut Pledger and 5 men. (Captain Dixon & Sgt Bunton since died of wounds)	JRW
	6/2/17	1 pm	Captain CHALMERS. 62nd M.G.C. took command of the front. 4 guns were withdrawn and trenches were re-organised	JRW
	7/2/17	11 pm	The Reserve section with reinforcements, mustering 6 guns	JRW

Army Form C. 2118.

WAR DIARY
or
INTELLIGENCE SUMMARY.
(Erase heading not required.)

Instructions regarding War Diaries and Intelligence Summaries are contained in F.S. Regs., Part II. and the Staff Manual respectively. Title pages will be prepared in manuscript.

Place	Date	Hour	Summary of Events and Information	Remarks and references to Appendices
			relieved. The guns, lewis guns which and came back to transport lines.	JpM
TRENCHES	11/9/17	noon 12	These Lewis guns were taken on conveyance on the night of the 7th/8th Sept.	JpM
			The company then proceeded by rail to Selles at RENESCOEZ by road transport.	JpM
			Casualties during action were 1 Officer (died of wounds) 4 O.R's killed 10 R's (died of wounds) and 14 other ranks 2 Officers wounded	JpM

Joshua Fry
Lt. Col.
64 M.C. M.G.C.

WAR DIARY or INTELLIGENCE SUMMARY

Army Form C. 2118.

Place	Date	Hour	Summary of Events and Information	Remarks and references to Appendices
RENESCURE	1917 Oct 8 till Oct 20		The Company were in rest at RENESCURE — the usual parades and ginnastics being carried out. Capt T.D. HALLINAN took over command of the Company on 13th inst.	
	Oct 20 Oct 21	7 AM 2 PM	The Company marched to ERBLINGHEM and entrained there, detraining at DICKEBUSCH, thence by road to camp near 64 Bde. Hq.	
DIRR x Rds	Oct 21 Oct 22	10.30 AM 12.30 PM	The Company paraded two 2 gun teams and marched by sections at 200 x interval to BIRR CROSS RDS where guides were waiting from 1 pm and 6 pm resp. The Relief was somewhat delayed through casualties to No 3 Relief but was complete at 6.10 P.M. The disposition then being as follows. Coy Hq. J.10.c.05.90 (2 Gun teams of the II Section) Capt T.D. HALLINAN 7/27 ATTER No 1 Section (4 guns) JETTY WOOD under 2/Lt RANKIN No II " 2 guns at J.10.d.80.90 " 2/Lt ADAMSON No III " 2 guns at J.10.b.90.50 " Lt. SIMPSON	

Army Form C 2118.

WAR DIARY
or
INTELLIGENCE SUMMARY.
(Erase heading not required.)

Instructions regarding War Diaries and Intelligence Summaries are contained in F. S. Regs., Part II. and the Staff Manual respectively. Title pages will be prepared in manuscript.

Place	Date	Hour	Summary of Events and Information	Remarks and references to Appendices
CLAPHAM JUNCTION	1917 Oct. 21	2.45 p.m.	No 4 Section (4 Guns) Returned to Guns of 63 Bry. being in Reserve then under 2/Lt ROWELL	
	21/22		During night Gas Shells were sent in vicinity of Coy H.Q.	
	Night Oct 22	5.40	Our Artillery put down barrage on right of Div. Sector. Practically no Retaliation	
			1 Gun at J.10 d 9.5 was moved to J.11 d 80.80	
			2 Gun at J.10 d 80.90 was moved to J.11 c 50.60.	
	Oct 23 4 a.m		Coy. Barrage was put down on our front. Retaliation light.	
	do	5.45	Our Artillery opened up a heavy fire. Enemy Retaliation heavy.	
			1 Gun was put out of Action (2 Lt ADAMSON) No Casualties to Personnel.	

WAR DIARY
or
INTELLIGENCE SUMMARY.
(Erase heading not required.)

Place	Date	Hour	Summary of Events and Information	Remarks and references to Appendices
In the Line	1917 Oct 23		During night of 22/23 Enemy shelled forward constantly chiefly in position at JETTYWOOD	
		11 A.M	Coy Hq. moved into MESSUS oufrees til then by 62 Bry. up till that time the gun equipment destroyed was 2 guns & 1 tripod. Casualties 3 Killed - 3 wounded.	
		6 P.M	Dispositions as follows:—	
			4 GUNS JETTYWOOD 2/Lt RANKIN	
			1 Gun √ M. 80.20 Lt. SIMPSON	
			2 GUNS JUDGE COPSE } 2/Lt ADAMSON	
			2 " √ II.C 50.50	
			3 " CLAPHAM JUNCTION 2/Lt ROWELL	
	Oct 24	8 A.M	2 Guns in Reserve at CLAPHAM JUNCTION were brought up under 2/Lt ROWELL & put in position at √10.8 30.20 2 Guns moved from √10 d 2.4 to √10 d 88 2 " √10 d 88 to √11 c 88	
			Ammunition was brought up during the night in bandoliers 10 S.A.A boxes	

WAR DIARY
or
INTELLIGENCE SUMMARY
(Erase heading not required.)

Army Form C. 2118.

Place	Date	Hour	Summary of Events and Information	Remarks and references to Appendices
In the Line	6/7/17	Night	Shelling continuous all night. 1 man Wounded. Dispositions as follows:— Bat. H.Q. J.10.d.00.70 2 Guns J.10.b.20.40 2 " J.10.d.20.20 2 " J.10.d.80.80 2 " J.11.c.80.80 1 " J.11.c.30.20 - " J.11.c.80.20 2 Guns J.11.d.80.80.	
		10h21	Nothing special to report. Our artillery very active chiefly against POLDERHOEK CHAU.	
		10h26 5.11.5	Zero hour for attack by 5th Div. on POLDERHOEK CHATEAU on which to turn guns on completing (2 at J.10.b.20.40 & 2 at J.10.d.80.80) firing barrage till Z + 120. Remainder of guns as follows:— Front line guns engaging any visible targets & 8.01 J.10.d.20.20 engaging low flying hostile planes.	

2353 Wt. W2544/454 700,000 5/15 D. D. & L. A.D.S.S. Forms/C. 2118.

Army Form C.2118.

WAR DIARY
or
INTELLIGENCE SUMMARY.
(Erase heading not required.)

Instructions regarding War Diaries and Intelligence Summaries are contained in F. S. Regs., Part II. and the Staff Manual respectively. Title pages will be prepared in manuscript.

Place	Date	Hour	Summary of Events and Information	Remarks and references to Appendices
1917 IN LINE	1917 Oct 26			
	Oct 26	6.10 AM	POLDERHOEK CHAV captured by Lt Duncan's Platoon. — 1 Gun out of Action at JUDGE COPSE J.1.c.88.	
			JETTY WOOD.	
			2 Casualties (Wounded)	
		PM 5.30	Barrage fire from 1ih 2+120 & then slowed up from S.O.S. Enemy put Barrage down all along front.	
	Night Oct 26/27		Spasmodic shelling all night. Enemy moving forward dawn. Enemy uneasy.	
	Oct 27	7 AM	Officer 237 Bry came up for reconnaissance preparatory for Relief.	
			Very quiet day. Considerable Aerial Activity. Many low flying planes being engaged.	
	Oct 28		The Company Relieved at dawn by 237 Bry & went to camp at HALLEBAST CORNER	

Army Form C.118.

WAR DIARY
or
INTELLIGENCE SUMMARY.

(Erase heading not required.)

Instructions regarding War Diaries and Intelligence Summaries are contained in F. S. Regs., Part II. and the Staff Manual respectively. Title pages will be prepared in manuscript.

Place	Date	Hour	Summary of Events and Information	Remarks and references to Appendices.
HALLEBAST CORNER	Oct 28 to Oct 31		The last 3 days of the month were devoted to getting the Company reorganised & cleaning up generally.	

H.E. Rankin Lt.
for 6/8 64 M.G. Coy.

Army Form C. 2118.

WAR DIARY
or
INTELLIGENCE SUMMARY.
(Erase heading not required.)

64th Machine Gun Coy.

Vol 21

Place	Date	Hour	Summary of Events and Information	Remarks and references to Appendices
HALLEBAST CORNER	1-11-17		The Company was out at rest at HALLEBAST CORNER. There was a Company Inspection by the C.O.	JMcM
do. do.	2-11-17		The day was spent in preparing for the line, fitting of belts, gun cleaning etc.	JMcM
	3-11-17	11 am	Two guns relieved 2 guns of the 237th Machine Gun Company in the front line at JUDGE COPSE.	JMcM
		9:30 am	The remainder of the Company paraded for the line. Guides were met at BIRR CROSS RDS. Relief was complete at 9 pm. Dispositions of Guns were as follows:— Company Headquarters was at H29.6.10".65". No 1 Section — 2 Guns in JUDGE COPSE, 2 Guns near REUTEL. No 2 Section — 1 Gun at POLYGONEBECK, 3 Guns at JETTY WARREN. No 4 Section — 4 Guns at JETTY WOOD. No 3 Section, In reserve at "B" Echelon. A Carrying Party of 13 ors. were handed over by the 253rd Machine Gun Company. "B" Echelon was situated at ANZAC CAMP.	JMcM
In the line	5-11-17		No 3 Section acted as carrying parties and carried up ammunition to Company H.Q. Rations for 2 days were carried up in the morning. Company H.Q. was heavily shelled.	JMcM

Army Form C.2118.

WAR DIARY
or
INTELLIGENCE SUMMARY.
(Erase heading not required.)

Instructions regarding War Diaries and Intelligence Summaries are contained in F.S. Regs., Part II. and the Staff Manual respectively. Title pages will be prepared in manuscript.

Place	Date	Hour	Summary of Events and Information	Remarks and references to Appendices
In the Line	6-11-17		Guns opened fire at 2 & 3 on Barrage lines and fired continuously for 20 minutes. 3 other Guns fired direct and obtained good targets. The S.O.S. signal went up twice during the day and all Guns immediately opened fire on their respective lines of fire.	J.W.
	7-11-17		Usual routine.	J.W.
	8-11-17		No 4 section relieved No 1 Section in the front line at REUTEL & JOOS COPSE.	J.W.
	9-11-17)			
	10-11-17)		Situation quiet and usual routine carried out.	
	11-11-17)			J.W.
	12-11-17		The Company was relieved (less one section) at dawn by the 10th Machine Gun Company and came down to "B" Echelon at ANZAC CAMP. No 1 Section was attached to 62nd Machine Gun Company from this date until ultimately relieved on the 14th by No 4. Casualties during this tour 2 ORs wounded.	J.W.
ANZAC CAMP	13-11-17		CAPTAIN L.C. BORTHWICK took over command of Company from CAPTAIN HALLIDAY. The Company moved from ANZAC CAMP at 2pm and marched to OUDEZOOM, arriving there	J.W.

2353 Wt. W2544/454 700,000 5/15 D. D. & L. A.D.S.S. Forms/C. 2118.

WAR DIARY
or
INTELLIGENCE SUMMARY.

(Erase heading not required.)

Army Form C.2118.

Place	Date	Hour	Summary of Events and Information	Remarks and references to Appendices
OTTAWA CAMP OLDERDOM	14-11-17		at 4.30 p.m. All ranks quartered in huts in Ottawa Camp, accommodation good. Weather dull & misty.	JW
	15-11-17		Day devoted to general cleaning up and reorganising after trenches. Employed on hut inspection which had been attached to 62nd Machine Gun Company reported at 5 pm.	JW
	16-11-17		The morning was devoted to cleaning up and thoroughly overhauling all guns, equipment etc. The Company attended Baths at Carvin Camp during the afternoon.	JW
	17-11-17		Preparations made for moving on the 17th weather improved. Company paraded at 10.30 am to march to DOUIEU.	JW
DOUIEU.			The Company arrived in billets at 5 pm. Dinners were served out on arrival. Billets were good, but very scattered.	JW
LACOURONNE.	18-11-17		The Company paraded at 8.45 am and marched to feet billets in the LA COURONNE area. Distance only about 2½ miles. Company arriving at 10 am.	JW
VENDIN.	19-11-17		The Company paraded at 8.30 am and marched to VENDIN Route - MERVILLES - HINGES arrived 4 pm after a good march. Roads were in excellent conditions.	JW

Army Form C.2118.

WAR DIARY
or
INTELLIGENCE SUMMARY.
(Erase heading not required.)

Instructions regarding War Diaries and Intelligence Summaries are contained in F. S. Regs., Part II. and the Staff Manual respectively. Title pages will be prepared in manuscript.

Place	Date	Hour	Summary of Events and Information	Remarks and references to Appendices
VERDIN	19-11-7		Billets and other times were good.	[initials]
	20-11-7		The Company paraded at 9.15am and marched to HERSIN Rants. BATHUNE – HALLICOURT – BARLIN, arriving at 1pm. Village was shelled on arrival, some shells dropped in close proximity to billets. Moved all men to front billets near H.Q. All were quiet after this. Rain fell during the night.	[initials]
	21-11-7		The Company, starting at 1.45pm marched to MONT-ST-ELOI, arriving there at 7pm after a very long march. Route. GRAND SERVINS – VILLERS-AU-BOIS.	[initials]
MONT ST ELOI			Men billeted in good huts with fires and very comfortable. Officers accommodation not good. Men being shared with 237th Company.	
	22-11-7		Day was devoted to settling down and cleaning up Camp which was in a very dirty condition. Guns & Equipment overhauled in afternoon also Company Parade out.	[initials]
do. do.	23-11-7		Morning devoted – Squad & Saluting Drill and Elementary Gun drill. Men very rusty, but should soon smarten up. Weather fine. The C.O. went to Division to meet Brigadier General CUMMINGS GOC M.G.C. went round and visited 256th & 237th Company in morning & 62nd Company in afternoon.	[initials]

2353 Wt. W2544–454 700,000 5/15 D. D. & L. A.D.S.S. Forms/C. 2118.

WAR DIARY
or
INTELLIGENCE SUMMARY.
(Erase heading not required.)

Army Form C. 2118.

Place	Date	Hour	Summary of Events and Information	Remarks and references to Appendices
MONT-ST-ELOI	23-11-17		2nd Lt Emmerard and Lt Buckell went round the line in the morning to reconnoitre the 51st Divisional Front.	JW
	24-11-17		The morning was devoted to usual parades. Games took place in the afternoon. The C.O. attended D.M.G.O. Conference at 1st Army H.Q. at 2.30pm, weather very gusty with little rain.	JW
	25-11-17		G.O.C. Bde visited Company in the morning, after which the Company attended Divine Service.	JW
	26-11-17		The usual routine of training was carried out, weather was very stormy. Football took place in the afternoon.	JW
	27-11-17		Inspection took place of transport by O.C. Divisional Train. Everything very satisfactory. Remainder of Company carried out the usual programme. In the afternoon a football match Company v 237th Company result 1-1. A Concert took place in the evening at the Y.M.C.A. which was a great success.	JW
	28-11-17		Usual training routine i.e: P.T. Gun Drill & Range Work. Inter Section Football in the afternoon.	JW
	29-11-17		Usual Parades. Inter-Section cross country run in the afternoon.	JW

WAR DIARY or INTELLIGENCE SUMMARY.

Army Form C.118.

(Erase heading not required.)

Instructions regarding War Diaries and Intelligence Summaries are contained in F.S. Regs., Part II. and the Staff Manual respectively. Title pages will be prepared in manuscript.

Place	Date	Hour	Summary of Events and Information	Remarks and references to Appendices
Mont-St-Eloi	30-12-17		Range Practice was carried out in the morning. The afternoon was devoted to football	JKH
		8.30pm	The Company marched to Savy where they entrained at 11.20am, fighting limbers only accompanied the Company, the remainder going by road to ARRAS.	

J.K. Macdonald Captain
Comdg 4th Can. Machine Gun Coy

Army Form C. 118.

WAR DIARY or INTELLIGENCE SUMMARY.

(Erase heading not required.)

61st Company Machine Gun Corps

No 22

Place	Date	Hour	Summary of Events and Information	Remarks and references to Appendices
TINCOURT	Dec 1st	1 PM	The Company detrained at TINCOURT at about 1 PM and marched to billets where they remained the night, half the transport joining at 5 PM.	
	2nd	7 AM	The C.O. proceeded up the line to reconnoitre it. The morning was spent in preparing for the line.	
		2 PM	The Company moved up to relieve the 164th Machine Gun Coy in the LEFT SECTOR. One section was left behind with Rear H.Q. which was at HEUDICOURT. Relief completed at 6.20 PM at W.21.a.50.95. TRANSPORT LINES at W.21.d.0.25.	
HEUDICOURT	3		Situation was quiet – weather very hard and frosty.	
	4		No section which was in reserve at Rear H.Q. was relieved at 3 PM by a section of the 237th Machine Gun Coy and proceeded up the line.	
	5		The section of 237 M.G.Coy proceeded to C.H.Q. at W.23.a.85.25.	
	6		One Section of the 62nd Machine Gun Coy relieved the section of 237 Coy attached and came under the orders of the 64th M.G. Coy.	
	7		Situation quiet	
	8		Situation quiet – Weather changed to very misty and a general muddle.	

2353. Wt. W2514/1454 700,000 5/15 D. D. & L. A.D.S.S. Forms/C 2118.

WAR DIARY or INTELLIGENCE SUMMARY.

(Erase heading not required.)

Army Form C. 2118.

Place	Date	Hour	Summary of Events and Information	Remarks and references to Appendices
	9		The situation very quiet. Enemy aircraft activity above normal.	
	9/10	7-30 PM	The company was relieved by the 63rd Machine Gun Coy. No.1 Section, under Lt HERBERTSON, who took over the Reserve position occupied by a section of the 62nd Machine Gun Coy, which was previously under the C.O.'s command. On relief sections marched independently to billets at LONGAVESNES. The accommodation was very poor, so the company commander was sent on ahead to improve the billets. The company was billeted in one large Hut and Officers in tents. Relief complete by 3 PM.	
LONGAVESNES	10			
	11	5 AM	A wire was received from the D.M.G.O. ordering 2 complete sections to move at 8 AM as the 11th unit to HEUDICOURT and the remainder of the Company at 10 AM, in anticipation of the enemy attacking. No. 3 & 4 sections with fighting limbers moved off and arrived at HEUDICOURT at 6.30 am.	
	11	10 AM	The remainder of the Company moved off and settled down in HEUDICOURT at 12 noon. The accommodation was excellent. Weather very cold.	
	12	6.30 AM	The company "Stood To" at 6.30 in case of hostile attack.	

WAR DIARY
or
INTELLIGENCE SUMMARY

Army Form C.2118.

Place	Date	Hour	Summary of Events and Information	Remarks and references to Appendices
HEBUTERNE	12		The day was devoted to General cleaning up. No man was allowed to leave the camp during the hours of 6am to 8am and 4pm to 6pm and were prepared to move at 15 minutes notice the rest of the day. The company was prepared to move off at 1 hours notice.	
	13	6-30AM	The usual "Stand To" parade	
		9-AM	One Section proceeded up the line to begin the work of building the new Company H.Q. at W23.c.5.3. The remainder of the company carried on parades under Section Officers. They were lectured during the morning on Trench Routine and discipline. The weather was rather dull with slight rain.	
	14	6-30AM	The usual "Stand To" parade	
		7-30	One Gun was mounted for A.A. duty. Parades under Section arrangements were carried on under Section Arrangements	
		2 PM	No 4 Section under 2/Lt ADAMSON relieved Lt NERBERTSON and No 1 Section in the reserve position on the Left Brigade Sector.	
		3.30	Relief Complete	

Army Form C. 2118.

WAR DIARY
or
INTELLIGENCE SUMMARY.
(Erase heading not required.)

Instructions regarding War Diaries and Intelligence Summaries are contained in F.S. Regs., Part II. and the Staff Manual respectively. Title pages will be prepared in manuscript.

Place	Date	Hour	Summary of Events and Information	Remarks and references to Appendices
HEUDICOURT	15		The usual "Stand to" Parade abolished & only one section to stand to in the future.	
		6.30AM	No 2 Section stood to under the Orderly Officer.	
			Weather still dull and inclined to rain.	
		9.AM	A fatigue party of No 1 section proceeded up the line to continue the work in new company H.Q.	
	16		During the afternoon Rugby Match took place — Transport V Company	
		6.30AM	No 3 Section stood to under the Orderly Officer. The usual Parades carried on under Section Officers. One section carried on the work at New Company H.Q.	
	17	6.30AM	The usual Stand to under Orderly Officer. Weather still cold & frosty. The Company made preparations for going into the line. Kit inspection. Cleaning & cleaning guns & kit.	
			The CO and 2 other Officers reconnoitred the line during the morning.	
	18	6.30AM	The usual Stand to Parade under Orderly Officer.	
			The company made final preparations for going into the line.	
		2 PM	The company moved off to relieve the 62nd Machine Gun Co. The dispositions of the Guns were as follows. 4 Guns of No 1 Section L.8 L.9 L.15 L.16	

J.H.H

WAR DIARY
or
INTELLIGENCE SUMMARY.

Army Form C. 2118.

Place	Date	Hour	Summary of Events and Information	Remarks and references to Appendices
	18		in the right REAR GROUP 4 Guns of No 2 Section L1.L2. L3. L10. in the right FORWARD GROUP. A guide from 62nd M.G.Coy met the above section at 62nd M.G.Coy H.Q. at 2-30 PM, and guided them to their respective positions. 4 Guns of No 3 Section L4.L5.L6.L7. LEFT FORWARD GROUP. A guide for the above section was at 62nd Coy Section H.Q. at W.23.b.2.1 a 2-30 pm. Tripods, belt boxes etc were taken over in conjunction with S.O.S and Battle Lines	
	19		Company H.Q was opened at W.23.a.5.3. Relief complete at 4.30PM. The situation was very quiet. Very heavy mist making observation impossible. Enemy Artillery extremely quiet. Slight M.G activity. Enemy Aircraft slightly more active, a number carrying our lines at intervals during the day. These were engaged by A.A. M.G's	
		7.30pm	A train passed company H.Q. in W.23.a, presumably to take ammunition, returning 1-30AM. Final S.O.S was sent up, but owing to the bad visibility could only be seen at a short distance, consequently only a few guns fired	
	20		The situation very quiet. Spasmodic Shelling of Bridge at X.25.a.2.	

WAR DIARY
or
INTELLIGENCE SUMMARY.
(Erase heading not required.)

Army Form C. 118.

Place	Date	Hour	Summary of Events and Information	Remarks and references to Appendices
	20/9		also the Sunken road at N.18.d.7.1. The Shelter of Gun Team at M.G.L.10 received direct hit, killing 1 man and wounding one. Our M.G's fired bursts at intervals during the night on VILLERS GUISLAIN and its approaches. Situation Normal. Our Artillery was active at 5.20 p.m. and 6.45 and at intervals during the night. Enemy Artillery shelled PEZIERES and SUNKEN ROAD N.18.a & b in Circles. Hostile M.G. fire was directed against RAILWAY in X.19 a and c.	
	21/9		Our M.G's carried out the usual indirect fire against VILLER GUISLAIN and New enemy work in X.14.d and X.20.b. Otherwise nothing to report. Owing to improved visibility during the last 24 hours, activity on both sides has been increased. The BRIDGE at X.25 a.1.6 was shelled at intervals and Tanks in the vicinity of M.G.L.1. The usual intermittent shelling of sunken road N.18.d Enemy M.G's active throughout the night, the bullets of 1 passing at a good light over VAUCELETTE FARM. Our M.G. were active against attacks to VILLERS GUISLAIN and new enemy works in X.14.d and CROSS ROADS	
	22/9		in X.14.d.7.1. Enemy Aeroplanes were active during the day and were engaged by our own A A M.G's. Hostile Aeroplanes bombed	

Army Form C. 2118.

WAR DIARY
or
INTELLIGENCE SUMMARY.
(Erase heading not required.)

Instructions regarding War Diaries and Intelligence Summaries are contained in F. S. Regs., Part II. and the Staff Manual respectively. Title pages will be prepared in manuscript.

Place	Date	Hour	Summary of Events and Information	Remarks and references to Appendices
LEFT SECTOR	22nd		The Left Sub Sector at 8.30 p.m. Artillery Activity normal on both sides during the day. Intermittent shelling with varying intensity throughout the night until 6. a.m. a.m.	
	23rd		Enemy bombardment from 5.a.m. assumed the nature of a systematic search of valleys or each Crests of VAUCELLETTE FARM and RAILTON RD rather than a Barrage line. VAUCELLETTE FARM and PEZIERES were shelled, a large proportion of shelling directed against the latter being "DUDS." Gas shells were directed against our Rear R'dos W.18.d. between 9p.m. and 11.p.m. Enemy aeroplanes active during day, these were engaged by A.A. M.Gs. 1 Enemy aeroplane was seen to fall N.W. of REVELON FARM at 4.15 p.m. Enemy M.Gs were active during intervals firing high bursts in the direction of REVELON FARM. The firing appeared to come from VILLERS GUISLAIN. Our Machine Guns were active throughout the night against selected targets behind the Enemy Lines. 2500 rounds being fired at Enemy works in X.14.d. and Cross Roads in X.14. d.7.7. Machine Gun at L.16 at W.24.C. 8.7. was withdrawn into Company Reserve	
	24"		Apart from intermittent shelling of VAUCELLETTE FARM the situation was quiet. Hostile Machine Guns were active during night on Front Line X.19.a and Reserve Trenches	JRW

WAR DIARY or INTELLIGENCE SUMMARY

Army Form C. 2118.

Place	Date	Hour	Summary of Events and Information	Remarks and references to Appendices
LEFT SECTOR.	25-12		at W.18.c.7.1.	
	26"		Our Machine Guns carried out indirect fire on MENDUER HOUSE, Cross Roads at K.14.d.7.7. THIEPVAL TRENCH, Cross Roads at K.15.a.8.9. Company were relieved by 62" Machine Gun Company less No 3 Section which was attached to 62nd K.G. Bn. Sections marched independently to HEUDICOURT. Billets in good condition. Relief was complete by 4pm.	
	27"		No 1 Section STOOD TO. Company paraded at 9am for funeral. Cleaning up & refitting.	
	28"		No 3 Section STOOD TO. The Company constructed dug-outs and sandbagged the billets in case of hostile bombardment.	
	29"		No 4 Section STOOD TO. Our Xmas dinner was held as one of the billets followed by a concert which proved a great success.	
	30"		The Company attended Church Parade. A football match taking place in the afternoon.	
	31"		No 2 SECTION STOOD TO. The morning devoted to cleaning up under Section Arrangements. C.O. inspected the Company in fighting order at 2.30pm. Redistribution of Guns in the line enabled No 3 Section to be relieved & the line Relief was complete by 4.30pm, Section joined Company at HEUDICOURT at 5pm.	[signature]

Army Form C.2118.

WAR DIARY
or
INTELLIGENCE SUMMARY.
(Erase heading not required.)

Instructions regarding War Diaries and Intelligence Summaries are contained in F. S. Regs., Part II. and the Staff Manual respectively. Title pages will be prepared in manuscript.

Place	Date	Hour	Summary of Events and Information	Remarks and references to Appendices
HEUDICOURT.	31st		No 3 Section held the Xmas dinner which was followed by an impromptu concert.	

J. Clotterbuck Lieut for Captain
Comdg. 64th Coy. Machine Gun Corps

No. 6.
MACHINE GUN
COMPANY.
No.............
Date...........

WAR DIARY
or
INTELLIGENCE SUMMARY.

(Erase heading not required.)

64th Company
Machine Gun Corps.

June 1916

Army Form C. 2118.

VM 23

Place	Date	Hour	Summary of Events and Information	Remarks and references to Appendices
HEUDICOURT	June 1/16		The company was in Reserve and the usual parades carried out. One section stood to from 7AM to 9AM. and the remainder of the company prepared to move at 1/2 hour notice.	
	2nd		The usual stand to. The day preparing for the Line.	
	3rd		The company relieved the 62nd Machine Gun Co. in the Left Sector. The weather was misty and the day kept quiet. Relief complete by 5PM.	
In the LINE	4th		The enemy Artillery was very quiet during the night. Lieut J.B. CUSTANCE M.G.C. came from mess Guiseppe sweeping our own L6 and L13. Our M.Gs fired on selected targets. Aeroplane active mostly ours.	57d SE
	5th		The enemy Artillery was active during the afternoon about 5 and 6 and M.E. & our shells frequently burst about 2500 Y's were active in fore part of the line firing on enemy Guiseppe Our M.Gs fired about 2500 rounds on selected targets. Enemy Aeroplanes over land dropping three bombs near Aerodrome.	
	6th		The enemy kept the line quiet.	
	7th		Enemy Artillery was fairly active Tanks leading to FAUCIENNES FARM. Cross Alt N.E. and CHAPEL CROSSING were shelled. Enemy Aeroplanes fired upon. Enemy Guiseppe near GONSET CROSSING and The Railway Embankment in X.13.a and the direction of FAUCIETTE FARM. Our M.Gs fired 200 rounds in X.5 SE.	57d SE
			The SUNKEN ROAD and X ROADS in 15.C and KILLERS TRENCH in X.9.a.00.	
			The FORWARD SECTIONS were relieved by Coy of No 120 [...] completed by 3PM.	

Army Form C. 118.

WAR DIARY
or
INTELLIGENCE SUMMARY.
(Erase heading not required.)

Instructions regarding War Diaries and Intelligence Summaries are contained in F. S. Regs., Part II. and the Staff Manual respectively. Title pages will be prepared in manuscript.

Place	Date	Hour	Summary of Events and Information	Remarks and references to Appendices
IN LINE	7		The Artillery was rather quiet; a few shells were sent over to CHAPEL CROSSING and FAUCEPETTE FARM. Several Gas shells were put down in N24a. E.M.G's fired on tracks from CHAPEL CROSSING to L13. About 4,000 bullets were about spent. Our M.G's fired about 1,000 rounds on the BEET FACTORY AREA. During the night 2 Airplanes came over our lines and dropped bombs.	57d SE.
	8		The enemy Artillery was very quiet. FAUCEPETTE FARM was shelled about 10-30 a.m. X13a was shelled with Gas shells. E.M.G's were very quiet. Our M.G's fired 6000 rounds on selected targets. E.M.G's very quiet.	57d SE.
	9		The situation fairly quiet. E.M.G's very quiet. Our M.G's fired about 6000 rounds on selected targets. The weather was very stormy & wet so was kept up but not observed by any of the gun teams owing to the heavy mist.	
IN LINE	10		Both sides fairly very active on the RAILWAY TRACK leading to BIRCH TREE COPSE and to Support Line on the RAILWAY. Roumptic Letting took place against FAUCEPETTE FARM. E.M.G. fire normal. Our M.G's fired 4000 rounds on selected targets.	
	11		Artillery fairly active. The 62nd Machine Gun Coy relieved the company. The	J.P.H.

WAR DIARY or INTELLIGENCE SUMMARY

Army Form C. 2118.

Place	Date	Hour	Summary of Events and Information	Remarks and references to Appendices
Line	11		Relay completed by 6-0 PM. The company marched to their billets in HUDICOURT. During the day guns had been lifted by the mules in reserve and guns were quite dry.	
HUDICOURT	11	8 PM	Our guns were mounted and put in reserve for transport during the night.	
	12		One Section stood to at 6.30 P.M. and was prepared to move at a moment's notice until 9 PM and the remainder prepared to move at short notice. The day was spent in general cleaning up.	
	13		The usual Stand to and Cleaning of Guns and gun equipment. During the morning the C.O. and Section Officer reconnoitred the Line for the Corps Defence Scheme. Enemy Aeroplanes active, one 8 Machines brought down in Flames.	
	"	10 AM		
	"	3 PM	A Fokkers attacked our Observation Balloon but was brought down in Flames.	
	14		The usual Stand to and the usual Training carried out. Two guns turned over the M.M. Guns in the RIGHT SECTOR. Relay completed 10 AM. During the day the Section Officer reconnoitred the Corps Line with the K.O.O's	
	15		Usual Stand to and Training carried out.	
	16		Usual Stand to and Training carried out.	

[signature]

WAR DIARY
or
INTELLIGENCE SUMMARY.

Army Form C. 2118.

Place	Date	Hour	Summary of Events and Information	Remarks and references to Appendices
HEUDICOURT	17		The usual travel to parade, and having programme carried out. Usual parades and preparing for the line.	
	18			
	19		The morning was spent in preparing for the line.	
HEUDICOURT	"	2.0 P.M	The Company marched off by sections to relieve the 62nd Mackenzie Crew Coy. The relief was completed by 4.30 PM. The Enemy Artillery was fairly quiet.	
LEFT SECTOR.	20		was very misty and actively quiet. The Enemy Artillery was fairly quiet except on Fronuois Killing against VAUCELETTE FARM and the Road near X.13.c (57 SE) SME. were fairly quiet.	
"	21		Our M.G. fired 2000 rounds on x Roads x.8.c 60.80 (57 SE) in front of VILLERS GUISLAIN. Enemy Artillery was exceptionally active on ROAD at N.18.c. (57 SE) and searching to 27.c. EME. was very quiet. Our M.G. fired 2000 rounds on selected targets.	
"	22		A great deal of work was done. Improving the Shelters and making new emplacements. Enemy Artillery fairly active. VAUCELETTE FARM was Shelled with High Shrapnel Enemy M.Gs. fired along the Railway in N.18 during the night (57 SE). Our M.Gs. fired 2000 rounds on Selected Targets, on VILLERS GUISLAIN.	
	23		Hostile Artillery was very quiet during the day. Enemy Machine Guns fired on CHAPEL HILL and CHAPEL XING. Our Machine Guns fired 1500 rounds on Targets X2d Lunetry and X Roads	

WAR DIARY
or
INTELLIGENCE SUMMARY.
(Erase heading not required.)

Army Form C. 2118.

Instructions regarding War Diaries and Intelligence Summaries are contained in F. S. Regs., Part II. and the Staff Manual respectively. Title pages will be prepared in manuscript.

Place	Date	Hour	Summary of Events and Information	Remarks and references to Appendices
an VILLERS GUISLAIN.	23rd	2a		
		3am	No 3 section relieved No 4 section in RIGHT FORWARD GROUP and No 1 section relieved No 2 section in LEFT FORWARD GROUP. Relief was completed by 3am.	
	24th		Hostile Artillery normal during the day except for very slight shelling against W.24.C. 70.80". Gas shells were fired at W.12.d. about 5.20am and again at 6.10am. Enemy M.G. positions on CHAPEL HILL were caught by our Vickers Gun fire during the night. Our Vickers Guns fired 1800 rounds on targets at X8d.	
	25th		Hostile Artillery fairly normal except against VAUCELETTE FARM, RAILWAY TRIANGLE and LOOP TRENCH. Enemy Vickers Guns fairly active especially against CHAPEL CROSSING. Hostile Artillery was active during some parts of the day shelling LOOP TRENCH RAILWAY TRIANGLE	
VAUCELETTE FARM.	26th		At 7 PM 2 white lights went up in the direction of CONNELEUX followed immediately by a discharge of 900 shells against REVELON and GENIN WELL COPSE. Later 2 lights went up from the same ground and the shelling ceased temporarily. During the afternoon an enemy Machine Gun was seen to fire at X.8.6. 50. Our M.G. fired 1800 rounds on NEATH POST beetroot grove about	

2353 Wt. W35/1454 700,000. 5/15 D. D. & L. A.D.S.S. Forms/C. 2118.

WAR DIARY
or
INTELLIGENCE SUMMARY.
(Erase heading not required.)

Army Form C. 2118.

Place	Date	Hour	Summary of Events and Information	Remarks and references to Appendices
LEFT SECTOR	27		Hostile Artillery during the day was extremely quiet.	
		6 A.M.	A few shells were sent over to H 23 & (57°S.E) W24 a and in the vicinity of RAILWAY CROSSING in H 23 a.	
			Our own Artillery owing to misty weather did very little or no firing at all. Enemy M.G's during the night were more than unusually active sweeping CHAPEL CROSSING and CHAPEL HILL, from the left of VILLERS GUISLAIN. Our own M.G's engaged GUISLAIN TRENCH in X8d and x Roads in X14 d. (57° S.E.), about 2000 rounds were fired.	
LEFT SECTOR	27		The 62nd Machine Gun Coy relieved the Company in the KSYR sector, the relief was completed by 6-30 P.M.	
NEUVICOURT	28		The morning was devoted to General cleaning up of Equipment etc. The Transport was inspected by the G.O.C and was quite satisfactory. During the day Enemy Aeroplanes were active, and 1 gun was mounted in the cart/s.	
	29		The morale stand to and a gun mounted for A.A. The day was devoted to General cleaning up of the men and camp. A working party of 1 N.C.O and 10 men proceeded up the line finishing the emplacements	

Army Form C.118.

WAR DIARY
or
INTELLIGENCE SUMMARY.
(Erase heading not required.)

Instructions regarding War Diaries and Intelligence Summaries are contained in F. S. Regs., Part II. and the Staff Manual respectively. Title pages will be prepared in manuscript.

Place	Date	Hour	Summary of Events and Information	Remarks and references to Appendices
HEUDICOURT	30		The usual stand to and parades. During the night Enemy Aeroplanes dropped bombs in the vicinity	
"	31st		The usual parades and preparing for moving to the new Area.	

J.H. Whittaker Captain
Comdg. 6th Corps Div. Train Cav. Corps.

10th K.O.Y.L.I.
Vol: 6

22ND DIVISION

22ND DIVL TRAIN A.S.C.
SEP-OCT 1915

(186 TO 189 Coys ASC)

www.ingramcontent.com/pod-product-compliance
Lightning Source LLC
Chambersburg PA
CBHW081542160426
43191CB00011B/1817